£14

The Aber Branch

Caerphilly to Senghenydd

Colin Chapman

The Author

A native of Llantwit Major and educated at Cowbridge Grammar School, both in the Vale of Glamorgan, Colin Chapman now lives in Leicestershire with his wife and family. A Chartered Town Planner by profession, he currently works in local government.

Colin was a founder member of the Welsh Railways Research Circle, the publishers of this book. His interest in the history of the railways of South Wales has its origins in the early 1960s in his many journeys by rail from his home town to visit relatives in the Rhondda Fach. At that time much of the character of the pre-Grouping railway companies remained intact and there was still plenty to see.

Four decades later Colin attempts to capture and explain this special appeal in his detailed studies of the railways of South Wales. This is his sixth book in the series and his previous works comprise:
* *The Cowbridge Railway, 1984 (now out of print);*
* *The Llantrisant Branches of the TVR, 1996;*
* *The Nelson and Ynysybwl Branches of the TVR, 1997;*
* *The Vale of Glamorgan Railway, 1998;*
* *The Ely Valley Railway, 2000.*

All were published by Oakwood Press, except *The Cowbridge Railway* (Oxford Publishing Company).

The Welsh Railways Research Circle

The Welsh Railways Research Circle brings together modellers and researchers who specialise in the railways of Wales and the Border Counties. The principal purpose of the WRRC is to put members in touch with others of similar interests and to go some way to avoid duplication of research effort. A secondary, but important, consideration is the publication of books such as this to provide an enduring record of the history of railways in Wales.

The group meets regularly in Cardiff and has a headquarters near Newport. To find out more simply contact the address noted below or vist the WRRC web site at

http://www.wrrc.org.uk

Copyright © 2002 Colin Chapman

ISBN 0 9527267 3 4

British Library Cataloguing in Publication Data.
A catalogue record for this book is available from the British Library

The right of Colin Chapman to be identified as Author of this Work has been asserted by him in accordance with the Copyright, Designs and Patents Act, 1988

All rights reserved. No part of this book may be reproduced or transmitted in any form or by any means, electronic or mechanical including photocopying, recording or any information storage and retrieval system, without written permission from the Publisher

Edited and typeset by Tony Miller, Great Gidding

Printed in Great Britain by Stylaprint, Ailsworth, Cambridgeshire

Bound by Woolnough's, Irthlingborough, Northamptonshire

Published and distributed by The Welsh Railways Research Circle, 22 Pentre Poeth Road, Bassaleg, Newport, NP10 8LL

The Aber Branch

Contents

	Acknowledgements	*iii*
	System map	*iv*
Chapter One	*False Start*	*1*
Chapter Two	*Promotion and Construction*	*8*
Chapter Three	*Rhymney Railway Days*	*14*
Chapter Four	*From Grouping to Closure*	*34*
Chapter Five	*Locomotive and Train Working*	*48*
Chapter Six	*Along the Line*	*62*
Chapter Seven	*Postscript*	*81*
Appendix 1	*Summary of Traffic at Stations, 1923-38*	*82*
Appendix 2	*Bridge and Demolition notes*	*84*
Appendix 3	*Extract from Rhymney Railway Land Plan, 1890*	*88*
Appendix 4	*Colliery notes*	*89*
	Index	*91*
	Sources and Bibliography	*92*

Acknowledgements

I would like to acknowledge the contribution of all those who have helped with the preparation of this book; in particular, Ray Caston, Tony Cooke, Gerald Davies, Richard Davies, Eddie Evans, Michael Hale, John Hodge, Bob Jones, Bob Marrows, Terry McCarthy, Brian Miller, Tony Miller, Dick Riley, Steve Vincent, Alastair Warrington, Ian Wright and many other members of the Welsh Railways Research Circle, Historical Model Railway Society and the Railway & Canal Historical Society, too numerous to mention.

Thanks too to my wife Diana for her help and forbearance.

Colin Chapman

The author and publisher gratefully acknowledge the following sources of photographs. The relevant Plate numbers follow each name:

Gerald Davies 1, 7, 8, 17, 18, 26, 36; D Greenman 33, 51, 67; Michael Hale 24, 25, 30, 32, 56; John Hodge 4, 28, 58, 60, 64, 69; Alan Jarvis 34, 49, 68, 72, 73; R W A Jones 2; LCGB 35, 39, 41; L&GRP 21, 22, 52; R H Marrows 53, 55, 57, 61, 62, 63; B J Miller 16; Jim Peden 10; Pope/Parkhouse Collection 9, 38; R C Riley 3, 5, 13, 23, 46, 47, 48, 65; M Rhodes 27, 50, 54; R Roper 66; Steve Vincent 5, 9, 10, 59; Alastair Warrington 31, 70, 71; Ian L Wright 45; WRRC 37; Author's Collection 6, 11, 12, 14, 15, 19, 20, 29, 39, 40, 42, 43, 44.

Insofar as maps and plans are concerned, the Glamorgan Record Office kindly supplied Figures 5 and 6 and the Signalling Record Society Figures 24, 26, 29 and 32. All other maps and plans were from WRRC members or resources.

The Aber Branch

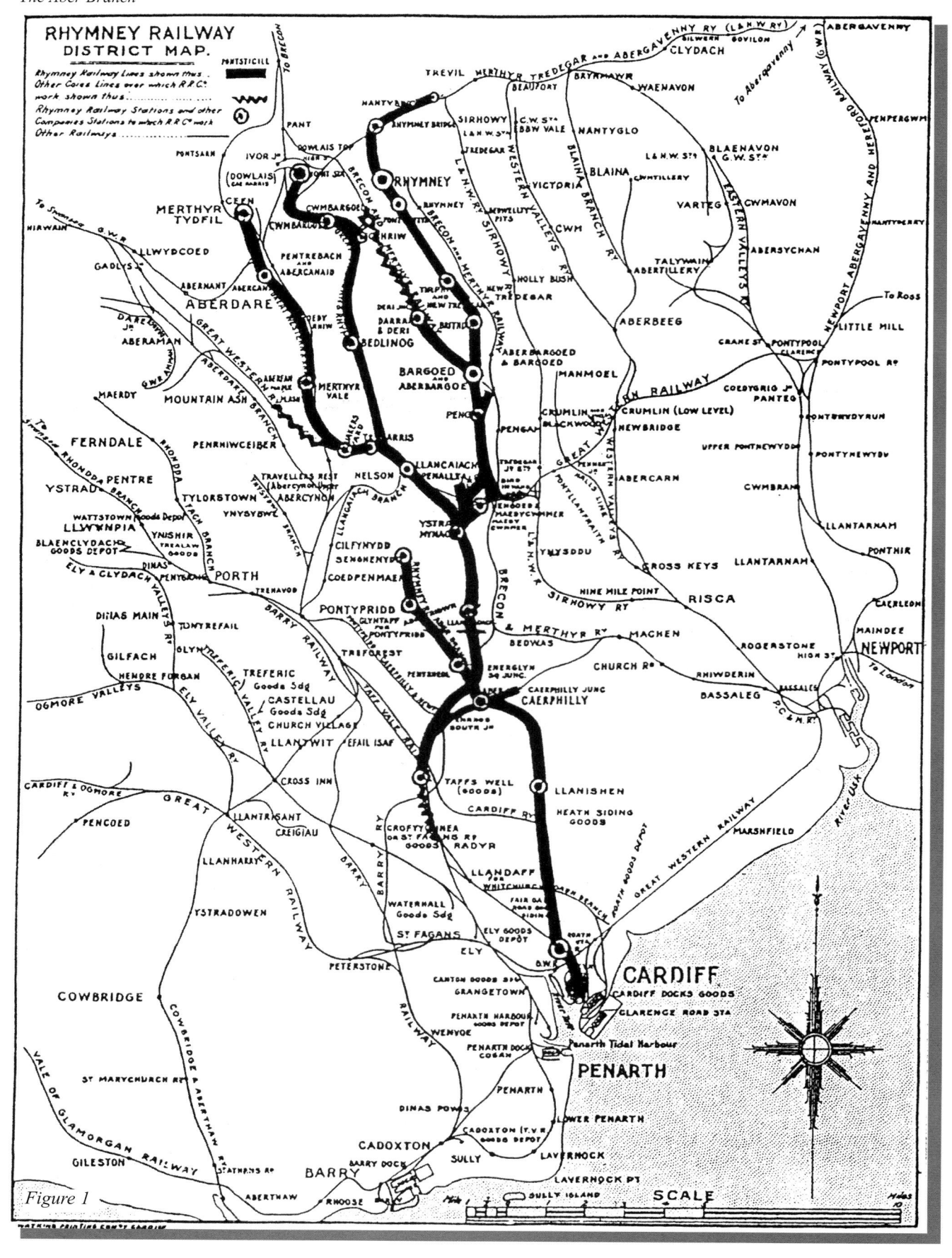

Figure 1

1
False Start

A very characteristic feature of the South Wales coalfield is the close-grained pattern of deeply incised glacial valleys that extend from its central and northern parts towards the coast of the Bristol Channel. By the start of the last decade of the nineteenth century almost all of these valleys had been occupied, to varying degrees, by railways, mines and densely packed urban development.

One valley, which, apart from a short section of mineral railway and two equally diminutive collieries near its mouth, had remained free of such intrusions, was that of the Nant yr Aber, a tributary of the River Rhymney, to the north west of the historic town of Caerphilly. After a false start in the 1860s, large-scale collieries and railways arrived almost simultaneously in this valley in the 1890s. In less than 30 years a tranquil rural enclave was transformed into a substantial mining community, with each of its two main settlements - Senghenydd and Abertridwr - dominated by a single large colliery.

Before embarking on the history of mining and railway development in the Aber Valley, it may be helpful to give a brief outline of the geological features which contributed in no small part to that history.

The South Wales coalfield takes the form of an elongated basin, with its main 'rims' formed by the 'Northern Crop', stretching from Abergavenny through Merthyr to Kidwelly, and the much more acute 'Southern Crop', corresponding to the range of hills running from the east of Caerphilly through to Kenfig Hill. This conception led early mining engineers to assume that the coal measures would be found at increasing depths towards the centre of the basin, with the much sought after steam coal proving uneconomic to work in that part of the coalfield. In reality, however, an upward fold in the strata - the so-called 'Pontypridd Anticline' - resulted in these seams being brought much nearer to the surface than would otherwise have been the case.

At the same time household coal found in the Caerphilly and Gelligaer Synclines, on either side of this geological feature, had been eroded away on the anticline itself. These readily accessible reserves were the first to be exploited, with early mines being sunk at Gelligaer, Caerphilly and Llantwit Fardre. Working the steam coal measures, on the other hand, required substantial capital investment in the form of deep collieries and represented a later stage in the development of the coalfield.

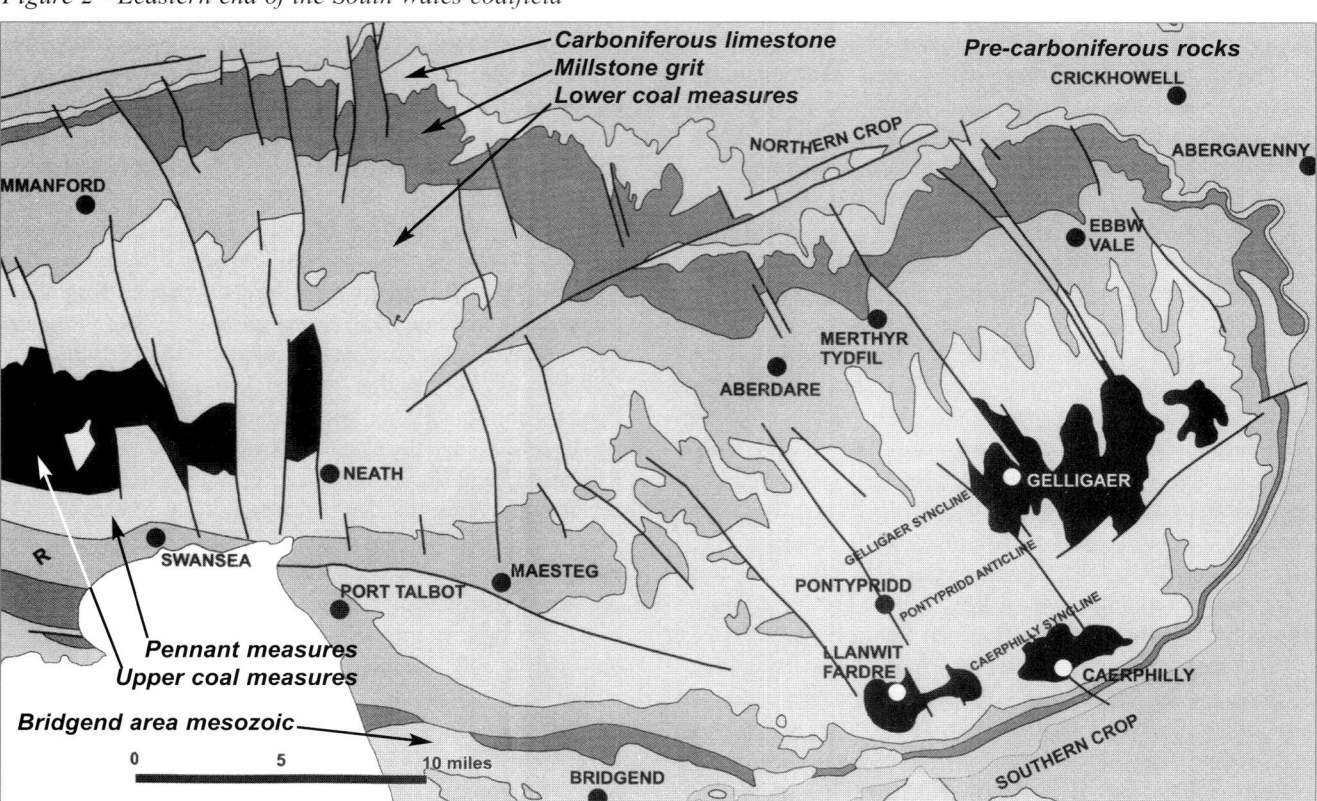

Figure 2 - Eeastern end of the South Wales coalfield

The Aber Branch

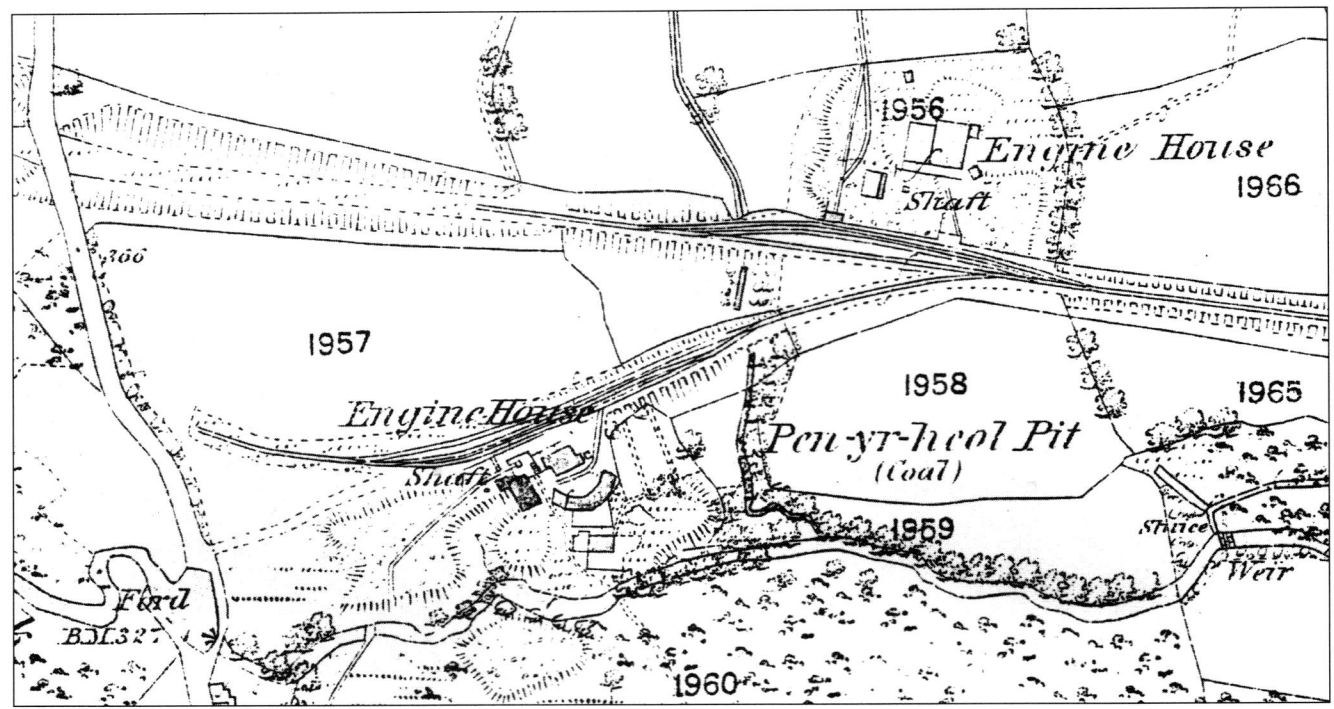

Figure 4 - Enlargement of the area of the collieries at Penyrheol taken from the 1873 Ordnance Survey map.

both Bills, was sceptical of the need for one additional railway between Caerphilly and Cardiff, let alone two. The prospect of both schemes being rejected by the Legislature proved a powerful incentive for an accommodation between the two sets of promoters, and under an agreement, dated 4th June 1864, the B&MR undertook to withdraw its proposed line in exchange for running powers over that projected by the Rhymney Co.

Faced with this arrangement the Committee relented and agreed to pass the Rhymney Bill. The resulting Act, which received the Royal Assent on 25th July 1864, authorised the construction of the new railway between Caerphilly and Cardiff, together with the Aber and Gledyr branches, and confirmed the agreement already entered into with the B&MR.

The Aber Branch

Having briefly mentioned the Aber branch in the above outline of the history of the Cardiff and Caerphilly project, it will now be appropriate to consider its development in some more detail. The idea for a branch up the Aber Valley had predated the grander scheme by some years. On 11th November 1856 the Rhymney Board, having considered an application for a branch railway to serve a colliery, projected by George Williams of Hendredenny Hall in the lower part of the valley, had given instructions for reference to such a line to be included in a notice for a Bill to be promoted in the following Session of Parliament. The resulting notice, which appeared later that month, included a proposal for a branch from the Rhymney main line at Beddau to Mr Williams' Penyrheol Colliery, but this feature did not survive to be shown on the plans deposited by the Rhymney Co. for the 1857 Session.

The idea was not abandoned entirely, however, as on 17th April 1857 the Rhymney Directors requested their Engineer, Joseph Cubitt, to prepare plans in respect of Messrs. Morgan's land on the 'Aber branch', with the company's Solicitor being instructed to serve the necessary notices on the landowners. On 13th June *Herapath's Journal* reported that Mr Williams was sinking two pits, one at Penyrheol and the other at Cwm-yr-Aber (near present day Abertridwr).

Anxious to secure a rail outlet for his new colliery, George Williams appeared before the Rhymney Board on 9th October 1860, only to be informed that the Directors felt unable to recommend to their shareholders the expense of constructing the branch line in question. However, by October 1862 attitudes had changed somewhat, and it was agreed to include an application for powers for the construction of the Aber branch as part of the Cardiff Caerphilly & Aber Railway Bill to be promoted in the 1863 Parliamentary Session. On 21st April 1863 the Rhymney Board resolved to form the branch as far as George Williams's colliery, provided the necessary land could be acquired. This proved to be something of a token gesture, however, as the statutory powers for this line were not obtained until the passing of the Rhymney Railway Act of 25th July 1864.

The Rhymney Railway Company's half-yearly report of February 1865 announced that the contract for this first portion of the Aber branch had been let to a 'responsible contractor' and completion was expected within 6 months.

A report on the project appeared in the *Cardiff Times* on 4th August 1865 displaying typical mid-Victorian ambivalence towards industrial development at the expense of attractive countryside:

'ABER VALLEY
The above beautiful and picturesque little valley is likely to become a very important mineral district. The branch from the Rhymney Railway, although slowly, is steadily progressing. It will soon be ready as far as Penyrheol Isaf Colliery, the property of Messrs David and Sloper ...Messrs Owen and James have also begun sinking a pit in search of coal at Garth Farm, between Abertridwr and Eglwysilen Church.'

Work on the new line took somewhat longer than had been anticipated in February 1865, and it was not until a year later that the Rhymney Co.'s half-yearly report was able to note that

'The first portion of the Aber branch had been opened for mineral traffic and coal was now forwarded over it from the Hendredenny Colliery'.

Further progress on the Aber branch was dependent upon prospects for coal mining further up the valley but there was little encouragement here as the early attempts above Penyrheol had not met with much success. Nevertheless, the Rhymney Co. was not yet ready to abandon the scheme. On 31st October 1866 its Board resolved to seek an extension of time for the completion of the remainder of the Aber branch, together with the nearby Gledyr branch, also authorised in 1864. These powers were granted in the company's Act of 12th August 1867, being for four years from the passing of the Act.

No further progress was made on either line, however, and on 9th November 1869 the Rhymney Directors were advised that powers for the acquisition of land were due to expire on 12th August 1870. This time reality had to be faced, and on 12th July 1870 the Rhymney Board agreed to abandon the Gledyr branch and that part of the Aber branch that lay beyond the land already purchased by the company.

Abandonment was sought by means of a Board of Trade warrant, under powers contained in the Abandonment of Railways Act 1850. The railway company's application for this warrant was a sorry tale of failed ambitions, with abandonment being sought on the grounds:

'That no collieries have been opened up in the district which the said branch railways now sought to be abandoned were intended to accommodate, and they being wholly mineral railways, there is consequently no traffic to be carried, nor is there a prospect of any traffic, inasmuch as the whole of the coal in the district is what is termed "deep coal", which will not be reached for many years to come; the reasons, therefore, which induced the legislature to authorise the construction of the said branch railways no longer exist, and your memorialists consider that it would be a useless expenditure of their capital to make the branch railways in question for many years to come.'

The application was accepted by the BoT, the warrant of abandonment being granted on 16th November 1870.

Meanwhile, despite acute financial difficulties and flooding in Caerphilly Tunnel, work had been progressing on the Cardiff and Caerphilly line. On 3rd December 1870 the tunnel was sufficiently complete for the passage of a train conveying some leading officials of the Rhymney Co. The new line was inspected for the Board of Trade by Colonel F H Rich, who, in his report of inspection of 25th March 1871, recommended that sanction be refused on the grounds of incompleteness of the works. However, the various defects identified by Colonel Rich were of a relatively minor nature and were soon remedied, with final approval being granted on 31st March.

The Cardiff and Caerphilly line was opened to traffic on 1st April 1871. It left the original Rhymney main line at Aber Junction and was laid as double track throughout. From Aber Junction it curved to the east to Caerphilly West Junction, from where it made use of part of the earlier Caerphilly branch as far as Wernddu, where it curved again, this time southwards, to pass through Caerphilly Tunnel and via Llanishen to Cardiff. A new station for Caerphilly was provided on the upgraded section of the Caerphilly branch, to the south of the town and adjoining the road to Cardiff, with the old one, just south of Aber Junction on the Walnut Tree Junction line, being abandoned.

Traffic growth following the opening of the new direct route soon put pressure on the single track main line above Aber Junction. Doubling from there to Ystrad (later Ystrad Mynach) was authorised in March 1872, the new works being reported to be ready for inspection on 30th June 1873, and was the subject of a favourable report by Colonel Rich on 10th July of that year.

The early 1870s saw a short-lived revival of interest in the development of the coal resources of the Aber and Gledyr Valleys. On the 7th October 1873, following an approach from the promoters of the Gwaun Gledyr Colliery, the Rhymney Board indicated its willingness to construct a branch to serve the latter valley. However, any decision was to be dependent upon the consent of the landowners along the route and Board of Trade approval for the revival of powers, and on satisfactory results from borings at the site of the proposed colliery. Landowners in the Aber Valley also pressed for the extension of that valley's branch railway from its existing terminus at Penyrheol. Unfortunately, in the absence of any progress with the sinking of mines to the 'deep coal', there was little prospect of either branch being proceeded with.

The Aber Branch

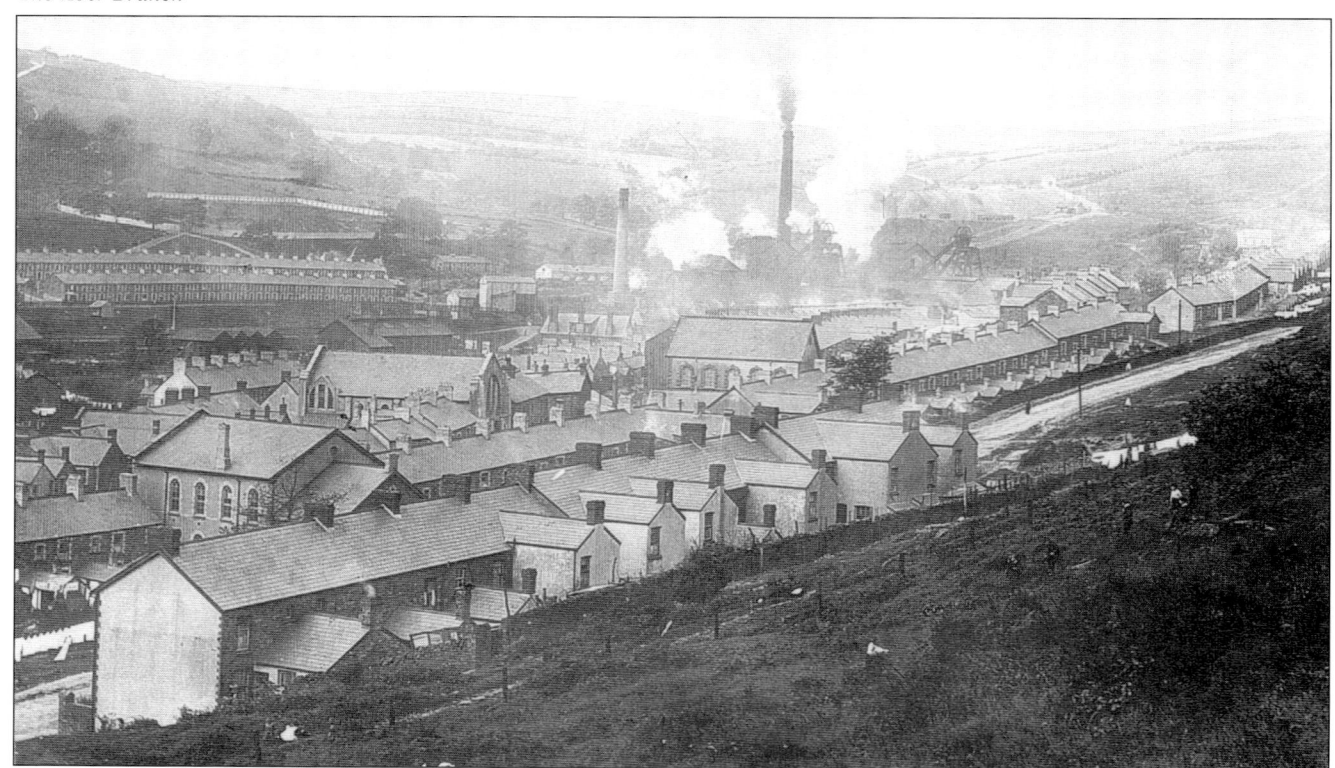

Plate 1 - Senghenydd looking towards Universal Colliery, c.1910. The roof of the engine shed is visible to the left.

Changing times ....

Plate 2 - Ex Cardiff Railway trailer No.142 and Class '64XX' 0-6-0PT No.6402 at Senghenydd in the early 1950s.

Plate 3 - A Down workmen's train leaves Senghenydd on 12th May 1952 with '56XX' No.6603 at its head.

.... at Senghenydd

Plate 4 - A very wet day at Senghenydd in 1963 after the line had been singled. A Caerphilly train awaits departure.

2
Promotion and Construction

The 1880s saw the start of work on two large collieries, one to the west and the other to the east of the mountains enclosing the Aber Valley. Both mines were intended to tap the deep steam coal measures which were also expected to be found above Abertridwr. In December 1884 the Albion Steam Coal Co. commenced sinking the Albion Colliery at Cilfynydd, to the north of Pontypridd and about two miles due west of the head of the Aber Valley, with the first marketable coal being produced in August 1887. By 1890 steam coal had also been reached at Llanbradach Colliery, about the same distance to the east in the main Rhymney Valley, production starting in 1894.

The sinking of these collieries provided a powerful incentive for the promotion of a similar enterprise in the Aber Valley. In 1889 the Universal Steam Coal Co. was formed, with a capital of £100,000, to develop a large colliery at the head of the valley. The moving force behind this project was the new company's Chairman, W T Lewis (1837-1914). Born in Merthyr Tydfil, Lewis had been appointed Agent and Engineer to the Bute Estates in 1864. For many years Chairman of the Monmouthshire and South Wales Coalowners Association, he was knighted in 1885 and acquired a baronetcy in 1896. He was elevated to the peerage as the first Lord Merthyr of Senghenydd in 1911.

Work started on the Universal Colliery in 1891 and by 4th December 1895 its Lancaster Pit had reached a depth of 650 yards, with five workable seams having been uncovered after 493 yards. The colliery became part of Lewis Merthyr Consolidated Collieries Ltd. on 1st May 1905, and in 1910 was employing 1,612 men and boys.

The announcement of the formation of the Universal Steam Coal Co. was followed by a veritable 'gold rush' of schemes to provide a rail outlet for the projected colliery, with the Taff Vale, Barry and Rhymney Railways all joining the fray. All three companies deposited plans for such a line in November 1889 for the 1890 Parliamentary Session. It will be convenient to outline these proposals in the order in which their Parliamentary Notices were published. The first to appear, on 15th November 1889, was that of the TVR. Three railways were proposed:

Railway No.1: from the TVR main line north of Radyr to the head of the Aber Valley;

Railway No.2: from Railway No.1 to a junction with the Walnut Tree Bridge branch of the Rhymney Railway, near Penrhos Junction; and

Railway No.3: completing a triangular junction at Penrhos Junction.

The Barry scheme, the notice for which was dated 18th November 1889, was part of a larger project for a direct route to the Rhymney Valley from that company's main line at Tynycaeau Junction. This was the company's second attempt to reach this objective; in 1888 Parliament had rejected its proposal for a line from Tynycaeau Junction to the Rhymney main line, just south of Caerphilly Tunnel. Of the railways now proposed, two are of relevance to our area of study:

Railway No.4: from Tynycaeau Junction to the Rhymney Railway at Penrhos Junction; and

Railway No.5: from intended Railway No.4 to the head of the Aber Valley.

The last notice to be published was that of the Rhymney Co. on 20th November 1889. This was to a large extent a revival of certain parts of the Cardiff and Caerphilly proposals of 1864, the main features being an extension of the Aber branch from its terminus at Penyrheol to the head of the valley (Railway No.1) and the Gledyr branch (Railway No.2). In addition, two curves (Railways Nos.3 and 4) were proposed to complete triangular junctions between the Gledyr branch and the Aber Junction to Walnut Tree Junction line, and between the latter and the Caerphilly branch, near Watford Crossing.

In addition to promoting these schemes, the three railway companies also petitioned Parliament against each other's proposals. However, the scale of the anticipated conflict was soon reduced by the withdrawal of one of the competitors. Under an agreement with the TVR of 19th March 1890, the Barry Co. undertook to withdraw its proposed Rhymney and Aber lines in exchange for running powers for goods and mineral traffic over the Penarth Harbour Dock and Railway (leased by the TVR) between Cogan and Radyr, and from there, via the TVR main line, to Walnut Tree Junction. The Barry Bill was then withdrawn, leaving the field to the TVR and Rhymney schemes.

The Rhymney case received a considerable boost when the company entered into an agreement (dated 25th June 1890) with the Universal Steam Coal Co., whereby the latter undertook to sink two pits at the head of the Aber Valley and the former agreed to build the branch line (subject to powers being obtained) to serve the colliery and to convey workmen to it.

The TVR Bill was subsequently rejected by the legislature in favour of that promoted by the Rhymney Co., the latter's Act receiving the Royal Assent on 25th July 1890. This Act authorised the construction of the four

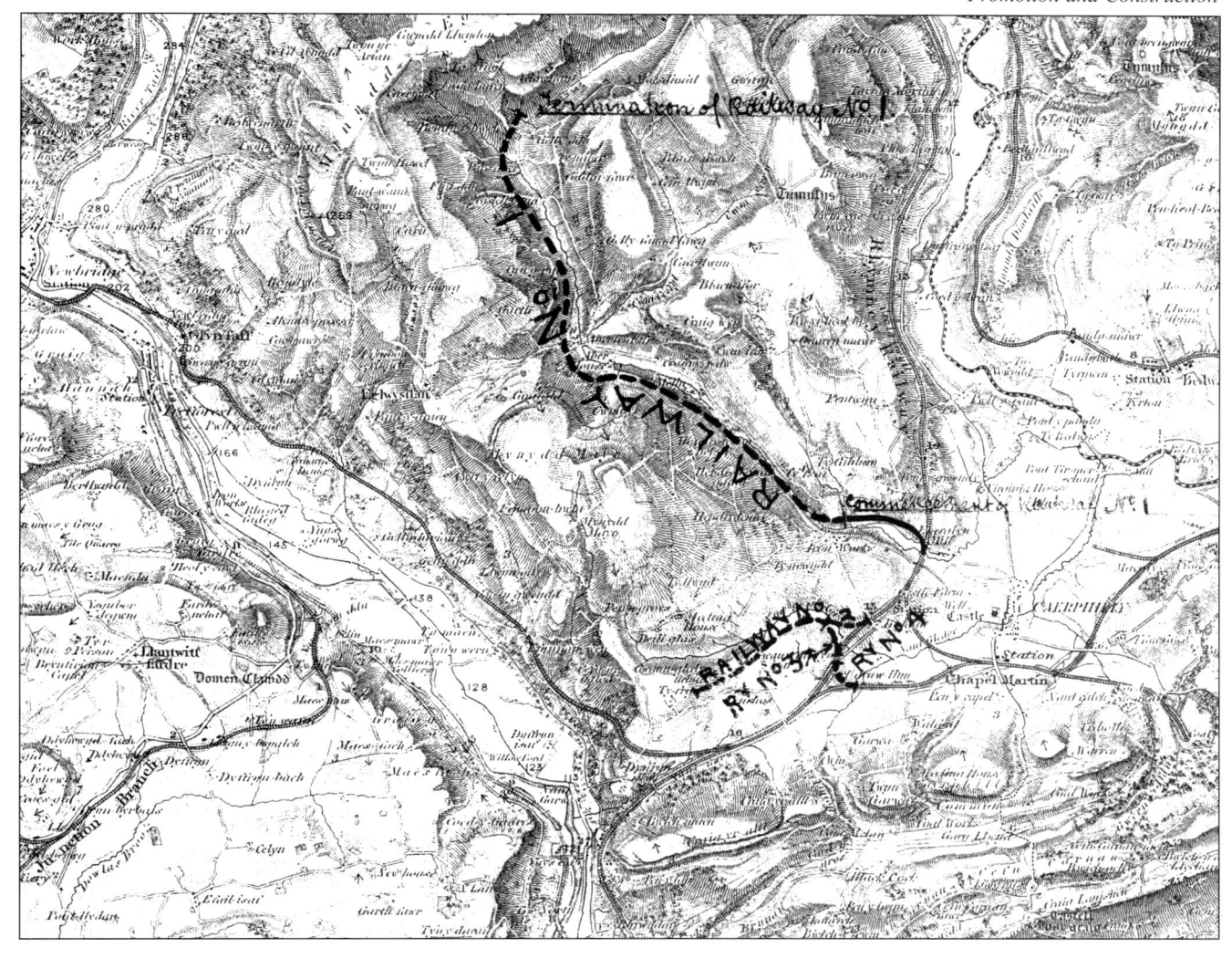

Figure 5 - The Rhymney Railway's deposited plan for the 1890 Parliamentary Session.

railways proposed in the Bill, together with the creation of £45,000 additional capital and borrowing powers for £15,000. Three years were allowed for the compulsory purchase of property along the route and five years for the completion of the works.

The Rhymney Co.'s commitment to the early construction of the Aber branch was not to be matched in the case of the other branch railway authorised in 1890. No attempt was made to start work on the Gledyr branch, the powers for which were renewed for a further three years in the Rhymney Railway Act of 30th May 1895, and then allowed to lapse. Fresh powers were obtained under the company's Act of 23rd June 1902, but once again no further progress was made, despite extensions of time being obtained in 1905, 1908 and 1911.

The remainder of 1890 was taken up with the various 'preliminaries' necessary before work could commence on the authorised railway. Additional surveys were undertaken, detailed plans prepared and landowners negotiated with. Tenders were invited for the construction of the line, and on 2nd January 1891 that of Mr T W Davies, contractor of Cardiff, was accepted for the sum of £30,421 4s 8d. Further progress was apparent when on 23rd January the traffic agreement with the Universal Steam Coal Co. was sealed.

A first hint of a problem that was to delay matters later in the year came on 6th February 1891, when it was reported that landowners along the route were seeking higher prices for their land than had been anticipated. The Rhymney Co.'s report for the half-year to 30th June noted that the contractor was *'using due diligence and making fair progress insofar as he is enabled to get possession of the lands required'*. Some very difficult points had arisen in the negotiations with landowners that had prevented the company getting possession of some important areas of land, something that was likely to delay completion of the work. Nevertheless, it was encouraging to note that many of these problems stemmed not from antipathy towards the new railway, but from the desire on the part of certain landowners to modify the alignment in a number of places so as

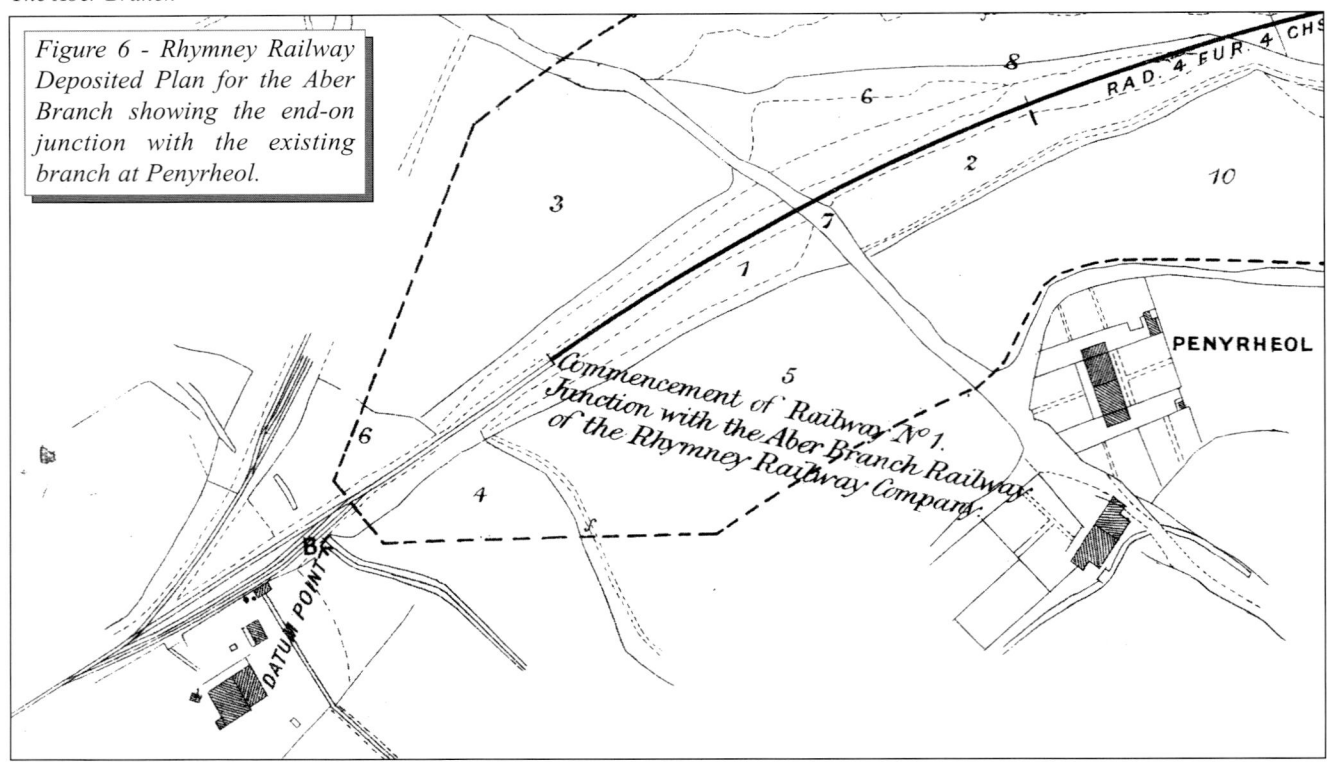

Figure 6 - Rhymney Railway Deposited Plan for the Aber Branch showing the end-on junction with the existing branch at Penyrheol.

to facilitate the subsequent construction of colliery sidings.

By the time of the half-yearly report for 31st December 1891 satisfactory arrangements had been made for the acquisition of all of the land needed for the construction of the railway. Unfortunately, wet weather during the autumn had disrupted the work, especially that involving the formation of embankments. However, it was expected that once conditions improved the permanent way would be completed on the section between Aber Junction and Abertridwr (some 2½ miles, of which a length of 1¾ miles was new construction). Above Abertridwr just over a mile of railway remained to be made. Here the contractor considered that within three or four months he would be able to complete a temporary line which would allow construction materials to be moved by rail to the site of the Universal Colliery. By the end of January 1892 sufficient progress had been made for the railway company to be in a position to seek tenders for the supply of rails, fastenings and sleepers for the new line.

The next half-yearly report (to 30th June 1892) recorded the completion of the temporary way throughout the length of the branch, with the Universal Co. reported to be making effective use of this new link to reach its colliery site. By the end of the year the permanent rails had been laid through to the colliery, improving matters still further as far as the colliery company was concerned.

The Rhymney Co.'s report for the 30th June 1893 announced that construction was very nearly completed, with the installation of the signalling apparatus and block telegraph being the principal works outstanding.

Unfortunately, this progress had not been matched by that at the Universal Colliery. The Rhymney Co.'s frustration over this state of affairs was clearly evident in the remarks (reported in the *Railway Times*) made by its Chairman, John Boyle, at the half-yearly meeting of shareholders on 11th August 1893:

'...it was a source of great regret and some annoyance that they had the line perfected for the conveyance of goods, but no prospect of carrying the coal from the valley for 2 or 3 years to come. He felt a little sore about that as the arrangement with the Universal Co. should commence from the sinking of the pits, or as soon as they could get over the branch materials and certain other things for their pits. This was not done with the smartness that was expected from the company.'

The colliery itself had been constructed in a largely uninhabited part of the Aber Valley. On 6th October 1893 the Rhymney Board agreed that the station at the end of the branch would be called 'Senghenith', *'which will be the name of the town to be built in connection with the operation of the colliery'*. 'Senghenith' was an anglicised version of 'Senghenydd' ('St Cenydd').

The Directors also decided, at the same meeting, to seek Board of Trade approval for the introduction of a passenger train service over the Aber branch. The new line was inspected for the Board of Trade by Major H A Yorke, his report of 30th December 1893 stating:

'I have the honour to report for the information of the Board of Trade that in compliance with the instructions

Plate 5 - The sylvan setting of the valley in 1893 prior to the sinking of the pits. The earthworks are in place and the buildings of Aber (later Abertridwr) station are well on the way to completion.

---

contained in your Minute of the 22nd December, I have inspected the Aber Branch of the Rhymney Railway.

This branch is 3 miles 34 chains in length, and extends from Aber Junction on the Main Line of the Rhymney Railway to the terminal station at Senghenith.

From Aber Junction to Penyrheol Sidings, a distance of about 45 chains, the line is double, this portion having been constructed some years ago (under the Cardiff & Caerphilly Act of 1864) and hitherto used as a mineral line only. The remainder of the branch is single with passing places at Aber and Senghenith stations.

The gauge is 4 feet 8½ inches, and the permanent way is of the standard type in use on the Rhymney Railway, consisting of flat bottomed steel rails weighing 80 lbs per yard, fished at the joints by plates weighing 22 lbs per pair, and fastened to the sleepers by means of fang bolts. The sleepers are of redwood creosoted and have the usual dimensions, and on the straight portions of the line there is a fang bolt on each side of each rail at every sleeper, and on the curved portions there is an additional fang bolt at every sleeper on the outer side of the outer rail. The ballast consists of broken stone and gravel and is sufficient in quantity.

The line rises continuously all the way from the junction to the terminus. The steepest gradient, which extends for over a mile at the upper end, having an inclination of 1 in 49.2.

The sharpest curve, which occurs at the junction of the branch with the Main Line, has a radius of 12 chains. Gauge ties are required on this curve.

Land has been purchased and the overbridges, cuttings and embankments constructed with a view to doubling of the line at some future date.

The greatest height of any embankment is 37 feet, and the greatest depth of any cutting is 33 feet; and both cuttings and embankments appear to be standing well, but they will require watching for some time to come, especially in the case of those which formerly shewed signs of movement. The works generally appear to be substantially constructed and the masonry to be of excellent quality.

There are six overbridges and six underbridges. The former are built for a double line of rails and the latter can be widened without difficulty should an additional line of rails be laid. Five of the overbridges and four of the underbridges, one of the latter having a span of 70 feet, are constructed of wrought iron girders resting on masonry abutments, the remaining bridges, both over and under the line, being of masonry and brickwork throughout. There is also a viaduct of three spans of 38 feet 9 inches each, constructed of wrought iron girders resting on masonry piers and abutments. The girders have sufficient theoretical strength and those under the line gave very moderate deflections when tested. It will, however, be necessary for the Company to provide outside wheel-guards on the viaduct at 2 miles 27 chains, and also substantial parapets or railings above the girders on each side in accordance with Board of Trade requirement No.20, and as the viaduct is near to a station, the parapets or railings should be of sufficient

The Aber Branch

Plate 6 - The newly-opened station at Senghenydd, with the Universal Colliery still under construction in the background. The site of the future colliery sidings can be seen to the left of the Up platform.

height to prevent passengers, who may, by mistake, leave the train while it is standing on the viaduct, from falling from the viaduct to the road below. In providing these parapets care must be taken to leave sufficient space between them and the sides of the widest carriages in use on the line.

There are three stations on the line, viz., those at Senghenith, Aber and Penyrheol. At the former there are passing loops with the usual signals and Up and Down platforms connected by footbridges, and the accommodation provided is ample and convenient. At Penyrheol there is no loop and no sidings and consequently there is only one platform and no signals, the line being worked on the electric train staff. The accommodation in this station is also sufficient. The signalling is satisfactory and carried out in the four signal cabins at Senghenith, Aber, Penyrheol Sidings and Aber Junction, which contain respectively 12, 14, 18 and 40 working levers, and 12, 4, 4 and 6 spare levers.'

Major Yorke went on to identify a number of alterations to the interlocking which he considered to be necessary at Senghenith and Aber signal boxes. Nevertheless, he was able to recommend, subject to his various requirements being complied with and the whole being re-inspected upon completion, that conditional sanction could be granted for the use of the new railway by passenger trains. Major Yorke returned for the re-inspection in June 1894, when he found that all of the necessary changes had been completed.

Although not mentioned by Major Yorke, it is worth noting at this point that the frames of the three signal boxes had been supplied by Messrs. McKenzie & Holland. The signals, as was standard on the Rhymney Railway, were of the signal company's 'somersault' type.

The conditional sanction of the Board of Trade, as recommended by Major Yorke, was sufficient to enable a passenger train service to be introduced and, in their half-yearly report for 31st December 1893, the Rhymney Directors announced their intention of opening the Aber branch for public traffic on 1st February 1894. They also took the opportunity to caution shareholders against holding out too much hope of an early return from this new investment, pending the opening of the Universal Colliery, but went on to note that:

'...for the conveyance of plant and machinery and other material for sinking, for housing building in the valley, and for the transport of workmen, also for what little general traffic in goods and passengers may arise in the valley, the Company's trains will be found very useful, and will be productive of some revenue both upon the branch and upon the existing railway leading up to the branch.'

The report concluded by assuring nervous shareholders that *'No trains will be run beyond what are actually required'*.

Promotion and Construction

(Right) Plate 7 - Copied from a postcard depicting Universal Colliery in its independent days, with coal wagons bearing the colliery name.

(Left) Plate 8 - Another postcard of Universal Colliery, a view enjoyed by the residents of Park Terrace, Senghenydd, c.1910.

Universal and Windsor Collieries

(Right) Plate 9 - An early view of Windsor Colliery, from yet another postcard.

3
Rhymney Railway Days

The opening of the Aber branch to public traffic on Thursday, 1st February 1894 was celebrated at a very early and, given the season, decidedly inhospitable hour. The inaugural passenger train left Caerphilly station at 6.30am, decorated with bunting and accompanied by the detonation of numerous fog signals. On board were about sixty passengers, including John Jones, the Rhymney Railway's Traffic Manager. More people boarded at Penyrheol and Aber, and the arrival of the train at Senghenith station was greeted by a cheering crowd and yet more fog signals. Later in the day a special train ran over the new line conveying Cornelius Lundie, the Rhymney Co.'s General Manager, together with several Directors and their associates.

Opening of the line to goods traffic also took place on the same day although, as we have seen, construction materials and stores had been worked over the branch to the site of Universal Colliery for some time prior to this date. From the outset, the rapidly growing settlement of Senghenydd attracted a worthwhile traffic of building products and shop goods over the branch.

The Aber branch's opening featured in the Rhymney Co.'s half-yearly report for 30th June, 1894:

'...the Aber branch was opened for public traffic on February 1st last, and both passenger and goods trains have been worked regularly over the line since to the great advantage of the district, although the traffic as yet makes no very substantial addition to the Company's revenue. The receipts, however, will pay the expenses, and by the opening and working of the Aber branch means are being afforded for the development of the resources of the valley, in which this Company is greatly interested.'

A substantial locomotive depot had been erected at the new terminus to cater for the large mineral traffic expected to be worked over the Aber branch and other lines in the general vicinity. However, this impressive facility saw relatively limited use at first owing to the delay in starting coal production at the nearby colliery.

Nevertheless, there were some encouraging signs of progress; at the Rhymney Board meeting on 9th August 1895 Cornelius Lundie exhibited a piece of coal that had been mined at the Universal Colliery. This sample was reported to be of similar quality to that found at Llanbradach Colliery in the adjacent Rhymney Valley.

The prospects for coal traffic over the Aber branch were further enhanced when, on 6th August 1896, the Windsor Steam Coal Co. was formed to develop a colliery just over a quarter of a mile north of Aber station. Promoted by James and Frederick Insole (owners of Cymmer Colliery at Porth in the Rhondda Valley) and W H Lewis, this new venture started out with a capital of £100,000, which was increased by £150,000 in 1900.

A siding connection was soon laid in the Aber branch, near the site of the projected colliery. The new work was inspected by Lt. Colonel H A Yorke for the Board of Trade. His report of inspection, completed on 27th September 1896, noted that this connection was controlled from a two-lever ground frame locked by the electric train staff for the single line section between Aber and Senghenith stations. The gradient at this place was severe, but Yorke was assured that it was the railway company's intention always to place the whole of the train in the siding before shunting commenced. The arrangements being judged satisfactory, Board of Trade sanction was recommended.

Sinking of the north shaft of the Windsor Colliery commenced on 3rd January 1898, with the south shaft following on 25th July of that year. Coal production started in 1903, the owning company having been reformed and registered as the 'Windsor Steam Coal Co. (1901) Ltd.' on 1st July 1901. By 1905 the mine was employing 850 men and boys.

After its abortive attempt to reach the Rhymney Valley in 1890, the Barry Railway made two equally unsuccessful bids for powers to tap the upper part of that valley by means of a branch from its Cadoxton to Trehafod main line near Pontypridd. The first was by means of the nominally independent 'East Glamorgan Railway', the plans for which were deposited in November 1893; the second was made under the ByR's own name a year later. Twice rebuffed, the Barry Co. decided to look elsewhere for a route to this objective.

On 16th October 1895 the company's Parliamentary Committee considered alternative routes for a line from its main line to join the Walnut Tree Junction and Aber branches of the Rhymney Railway, and agreed to make a fresh attempt with the scheme first proposed in the 1890 Session. This time, however, the Barry scheme proved more successful, the Act receiving the Royal Assent on 7th August 1896. The two railways forming the link to the Rhymney Railway were:

Railway No.1: From the ByR main line at Tynycaeau Junction to the Rhymney Railway at Penrhos Junction;
and
Railway No.2: From Railway No.1 near Penrhos Junction to a junction with the Aber branch.

The Act also granted running powers for Barry Railway passenger trains from Penrhos Junction into Caerphilly station. Goods and mineral traffic, on the other hand, would have to be exchanged at any junctions with the Rhymney Railway.

Railway No.1 was opened to traffic on 1st August 1901, the first train consisting of thirty-three wagons loaded with coal from the Deep Navigation Colliery at Treharris. However, no attempt was made to start work on the authorised connection to the Aber branch. Without running powers over the latter such a line would have been of little use. Similar powers over the Rhymney Railway, north of Penrhos Junction, had been sought in the 1897 Session, but had been withdrawn before it came before Committee. Consideration was also given to the construction of an independent extension up the Aber Valley to the Windsor Colliery, this proposal being outlined in a report prepared by James Bell, the ByR Engineer, on 1st May 1901.

Bell had been over the route with his General Manager and a number of the Directors on 12th April, and had also taken levels and prepared an estimate of the cost of the line. At £35,000, its high cost reflected the value of the building land that would need to be acquired along the route proposed. However, nothing more was heard of this suggested branch. Extensions of time for the Barry Co.'s authorised connection to the Aber branch were obtained on 26th July 1901 and 11th August 1903 (on both occasions for two years), but the powers were then allowed to lapse.

A Successful Barry Scheme

Another scheme for an extension from the ByR's Rhymney branch proved somewhat more successful. On 25th July 1898 the Barry Co. obtained powers for a line from near Penrhos Junction to a junction with the Brecon & Merthyr Railway, north of Bedwas. This proposal made use of part of the authorised route of the connection to the Aber branch, but without prejudicing its eventual construction. It crossed the Aber Valley and its railway, about 370 yards east of Penyrheol station, by means of Penyrheol Viaduct, 380 yards long, consisting of four arches, ten plate-girder spans and four lattice-girder spans (each of 100 feet) resting on brick-built piers. This line was opened to goods and mineral traffic on 2nd January 1905 but the B&M Directors' Minute of 4th January notes that the junction with the Rhymney Railway at Energlyn was incomplete.

The advent of coal traffic off the Aber branch, coupled with the continuing increase in the volume handled on the Rhymney main line, led to the need for improvements in the accommodation provided at Aber Junction. On 2nd April 1897 the tender of James Allen was accepted for the construction of reception sidings at the junction. A new Down relief line between Pwllypant and Aber Junction was authorised on 1st April 1898, James Allen once again succeeding with his tender bid. The Board of Trade inspection was carried out by Lt. Colonel H A Yorke, whose report of 21st June 1899 recommended approval for the new arrangements. The new line commenced at Pwllypant Signal Box and continued past Aber Junction to rejoin the Caerphilly line just beyond the junction with the Walnut Tree Junction branch. It was to be used by Down passenger trains, the old line being given over to Down goods and mineral traffic.

The Aber Junction to Penrhos Junction line, which had remained single track, was expected to see a considerable increase in its traffic following the opening of the Rhymney branch of the ByR. On 10th February 1899 authority was given to double this section, at an estimated cost of £2,700-£3,000. The rest of this branch, from Penrhos Junction to Walnut Tree Junction, stayed as a single line.

Prior to the building of the railway a tiny hamlet at Cwm-yr-Aber was the only settlement of any consequence in the Aber Valley. The development of the Windsor Colliery brought with it the need for accommodation for the incoming miners, and by 1898 rows of pennant grit terraces had been erected to the west of Aber station (Tridwr Road) and along the main road to Senghenydd. On 2nd June 1899 the Rhymney Board accepted the suggestion of the Aber Station Master that his station be renamed 'Abertridwr' (meaning the confluence of three streams), the name by then used for the adjoining village. This renaming was effective from 26th June.

Development at Abertridwr proceeded apace and by 1906 over 500 houses had been built, with a further 200 being added over the next four years, the village's population reaching 4,500 persons in 1910. By 1915 this settlement had all but merged with that of Senghenydd, ribbon development being almost continuous along the Senghenydd Road (*overleaf*).

It will be recalled that the layout at Senghenith station comprised a short length of double line, with Up and Down platforms, with the single line continuing beyond to provide access to the Universal Colliery. Unfortunately, this arrangement did not prove to be a convenient one for passenger trains, which, having arrived at the Up platform, then had to be shunted across to the Down line before departing for Caerphilly. To avoid the need for this time-consuming and wasteful manoeuvre it was proposed to alter the signalling to allow these trains to arrive at and then depart from the Down platform.

The re-arrangement was reported to be ready for inspection on 12th September 1901, and was inspected for the Board of Trade by Major E Druitt, whose report, completed on 31st October, stated:

'Senghenith Station is the terminus for passenger traffic on this branch line, and though there is a loop at the station and two platforms, it is desired to run trains into the station on the Down platform road instead of the Up, so as to be ready to depart again almost at once.

Accordingly, the Down line has been signalled for both arrival and departure, an additional signal for running into the Down platform having been now

The Aber Branch

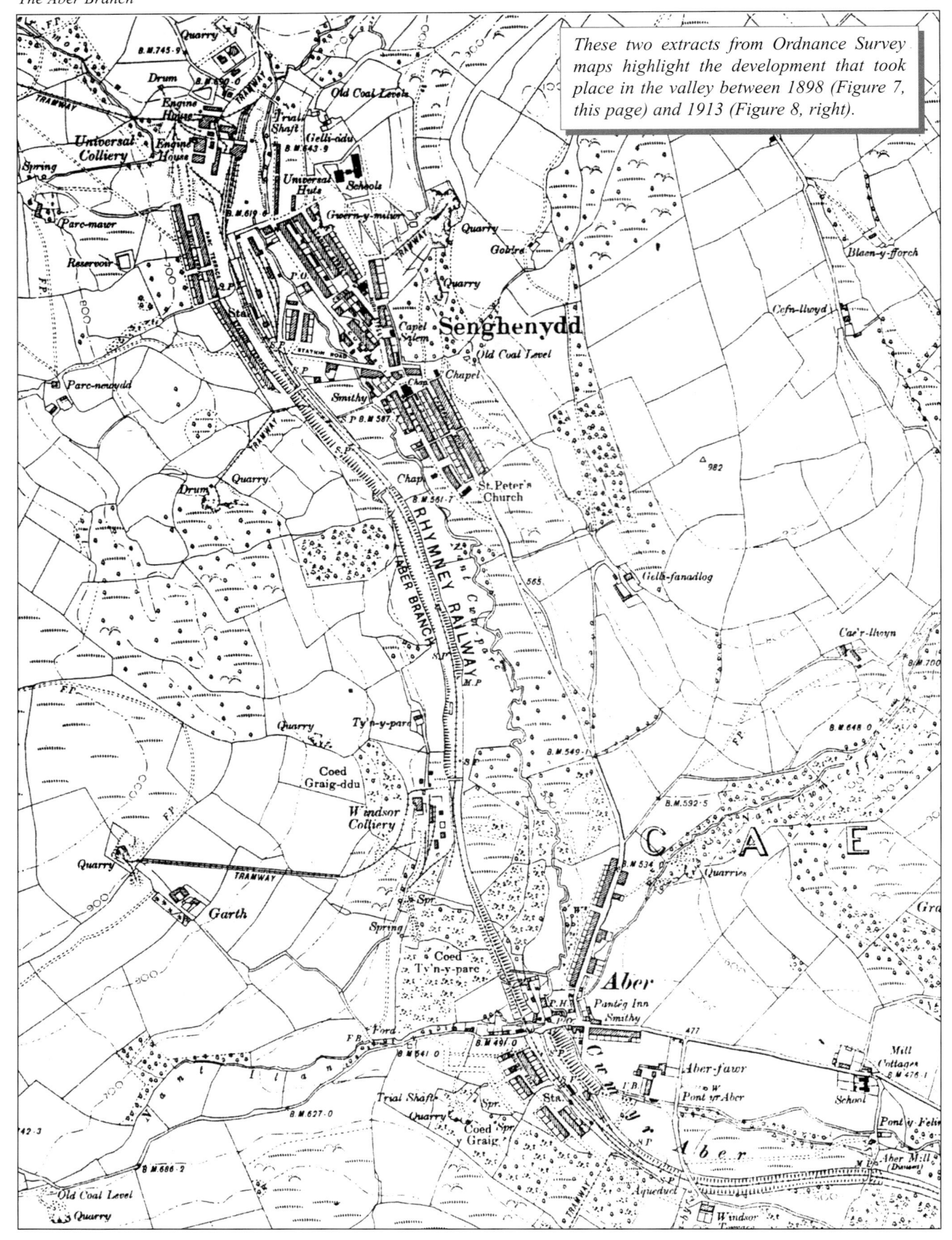

These two extracts from Ordnance Survey maps highlight the development that took place in the valley between 1898 (Figure 7, this page) and 1913 (Figure 8, right).

16

Rhymney Railway Days

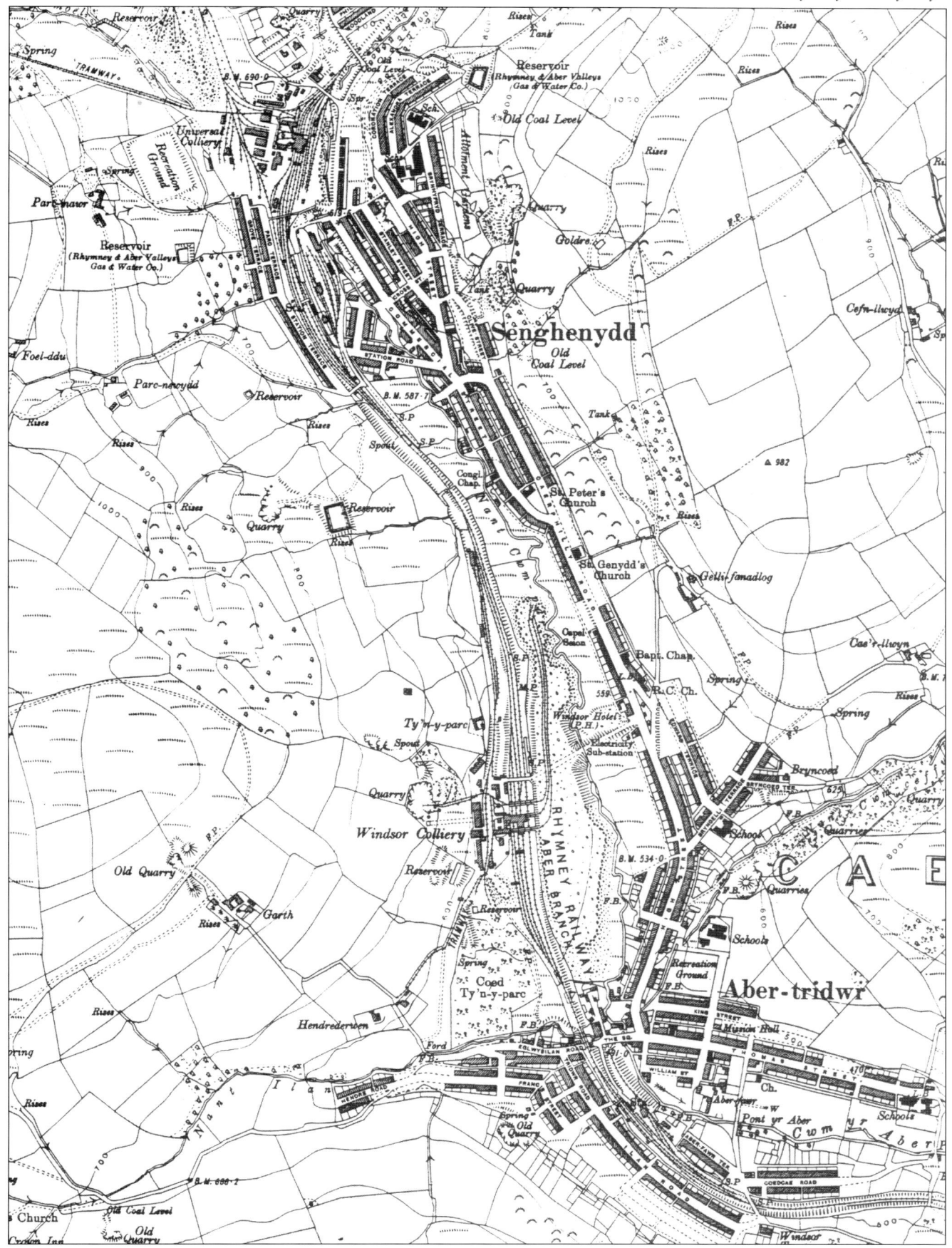

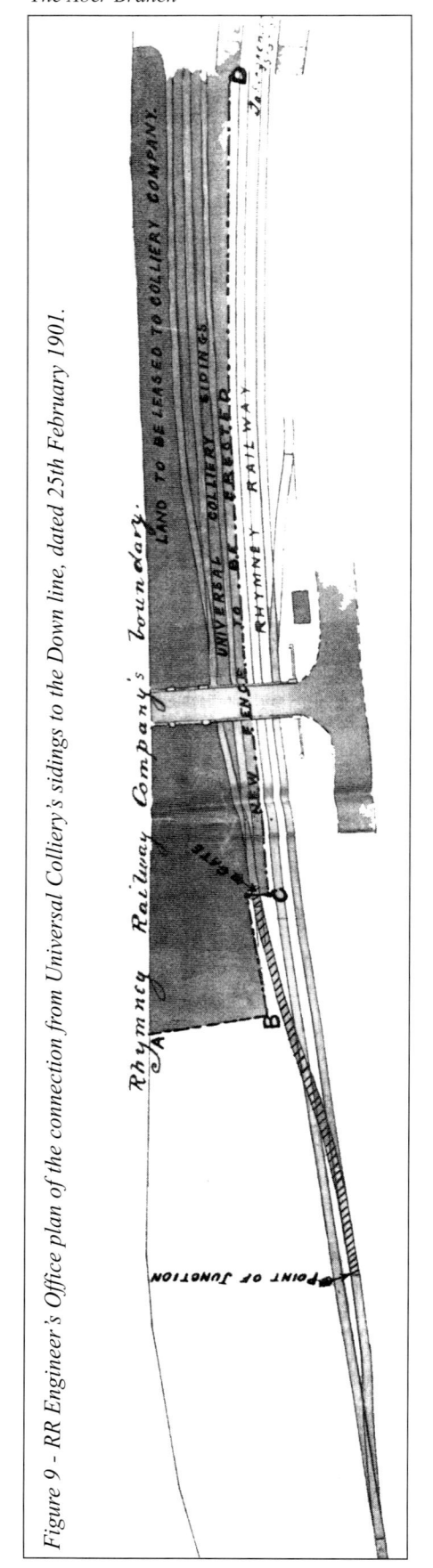

The Aber Branch

Figure 9 - RR Engineer's Office plan of the connection from Universal Colliery's sidings to the Down line, dated 25th February 1901.

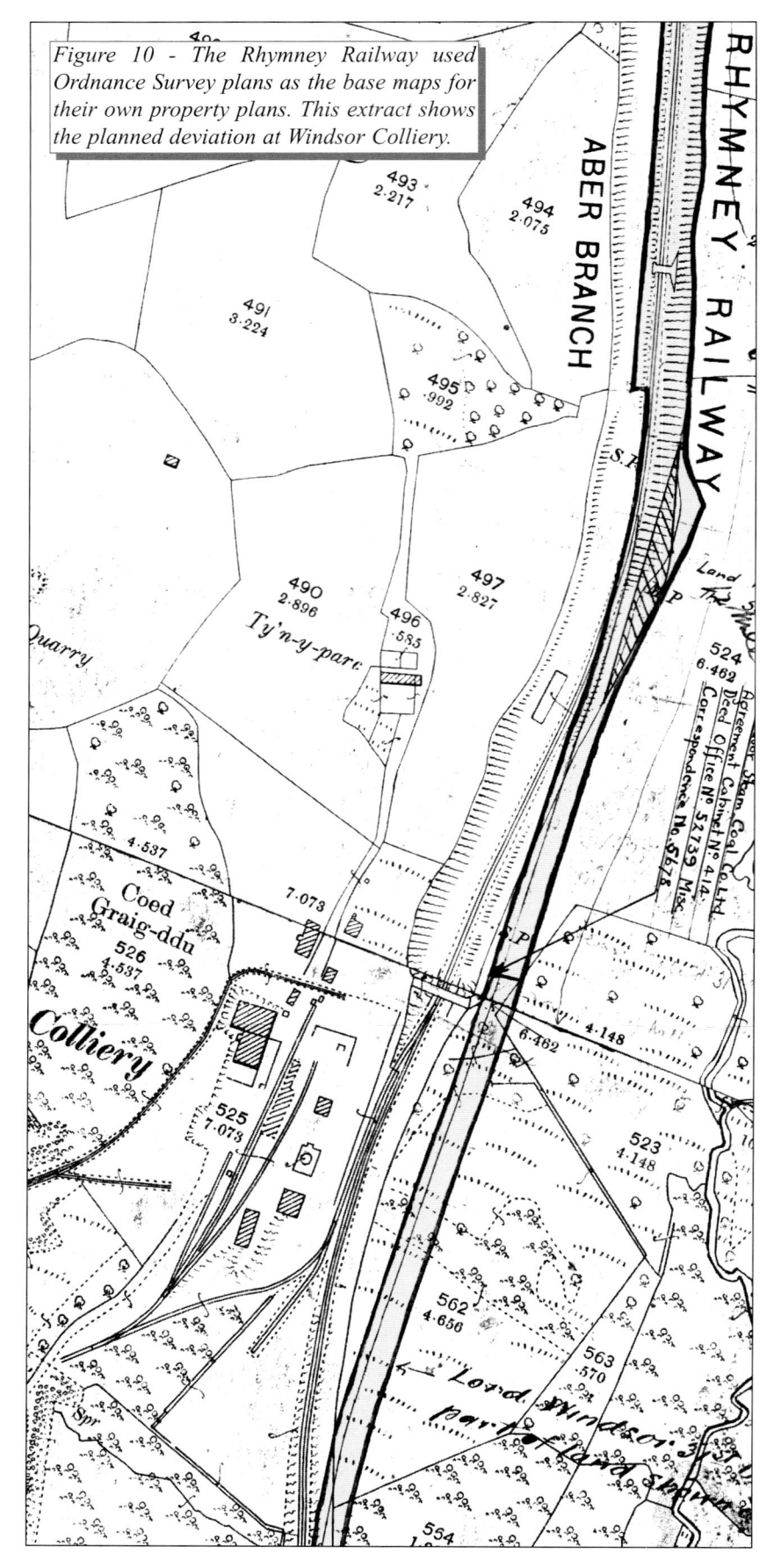

Figure 10 - The Rhymney Railway used Ordnance Survey plans as the base maps for their own property plans. This extract shows the planned deviation at Windsor Colliery.

Plate 10 - Senghenydd station and Universal Colliery from a postcard postmarked 7th October 1907. Comparison with Plate 6 shows that the 'loaded' coal sidings have been built on the Up side of the line. The goods yard is being shunted by one of the company's saddle tanks and there are three brake vans stabled on the van siding awaiting work.

added; and also an Up starting signal at the top end of the Down platform to be used only for an engine running round its train. The Down platform line is to be used in the Up direction only for passenger traffic.

The use of the Down line in the above manner can only be sanctioned on condition that no carriages are left standing on it at the station, without an engine attached, for longer than is just necessary for an engine to run round the train, as there are no trap points at the bottom of the loop in the Down line, and the gradient is steep.'

In addition, a new trailing connection had been provided (under an agreement with the colliery company of 18th March 1901) to the Down line from newly laid loaded wagon sidings on the Up side of the line.*(Fig.9)* Land had been levelled for these sidings when the railway had been built, but construction only became necessary when coal began to be despatched in earnest from the Universal Colliery. Empty wagons continued to be worked into the colliery yard by means of the upper siding connection. The signal box now contained 19 working and 5 spare levers.

Major Druitt was satisfied with the new arrangements, subject to the requirement mentioned in the above extract from his report of inspection, and recommended that the Board of Trade sanction the use of the new works.

The start of coal production at Windsor Colliery also necessitated revisions to siding arrangements to cope with the additional traffic. The original siding connection was removed and a new alignment *(Fig.10)*, about a quarter of a mile long, was constructed to the east of the old one under an agreement (dated 16th April 1903) between the railway company and the Windsor Steam Coal Co. (1901) Ltd. This alteration produced extra space for new colliery sidings and screens. A new connection, facing for Up trains, was laid in the single line, nearer Abertridwr station, to serve this bank of sidings. This was reported to be ready for inspection on 28th May 1903, the provisional sanction of the Board of Trade being granted on 3rd June. Major Druitt returned to the Aber Valley, completing his report of inspection on 15th July. The new siding connection was controlled by a two-lever ground frame, locked by the electric train staff for the section of line between Abertridwr and Senghenith stations, an arrangement which was approved of by Major Druitt. An upper siding connection, under the control of Windsor Colliery North ground frame, was also provided.

A further station renaming was agreed on 1st July 1904, when the Rhymney Directors decided that the branch terminus should be re-titled 'Senghenydd' to bring it into line with the spelling by then used for the village that had sprung up at the head of the Aber Valley. According to Railway Clearing House records this change of name was

The Aber Branch

Plate 11 - A pre-grouping view of Senghenydd station, looking towards the Universal Colliery. Note the passenger coaches stabled in the siding alongside the goods shed road to the extreme right of the picture.

effective from the date of the Board meeting.

The village itself was by now a substantial mining community, but one that had already suffered the first of two savage blows from the same source. On 24th May 1901, 81 miners had been killed in an underground explosion at the Universal Colliery.

Major Works

The opening of the Rhymney branch of the Barry Railway, coupled with the growth of the coal output of the Aber Valley and other parts of the Rhymney system, increased the pressure on Aber Junction, by now the hub of the Rhymney Railway's mineral traffic operations. Following their inspection of the line on 24th July 1903, the Rhymney Directors agreed, at their meeting on 6th August, to the carrying out of substantial improvements at the junction. The tender of Messrs. McKenzie & Holland for the signalling work was accepted on 2nd October, followed, on 6th November, by that of W A Symes for the masonry and earthworks. However, these decisions were soon overtaken by proposals for a further raft of major improvements, sanctioned by the Rhymney Board on 8th April 1904. These comprised:

* A fourth line between Pwllypant and Aber Junction;
* New interchange sidings on the Walnut Tree Junction branch south of Aber Junction;
* A new curve between the Walnut Tree Junction branch and the Caerphilly branch (the 'Beddau Loop');
* Doubling of the Caerphilly branch between Penrhos Junction and Caerphilly West Junction; *and*
* New Up sidings at Aber Junction.

Taken together, these measures would considerably improve the working of mineral traffic over the lines focussing on Aber Junction at an estimated cost of £24,200. On 2nd December 1904 the Rhymney Board accepted the tender of T W Davies for the new works at Aber Junction, together with the new storage sidings, for the sum of £6,383 19s 11d.

Board of Trade approval for the new arrangements was sought on 16th November 1905. Once again, the inspection was carried out by E Druitt (by now a Lt. Colonel in the Royal Engineers), who found that substantial alterations had been carried out at Aber Junction. There were now two pairs of running lines - Up and Down mineral to the east and Up and Down passenger to the west - between Pwllypant and Aber Junction, with the passenger lines avoiding the complex of junctions at the latter place. The Aber branch now joined the mineral lines, the passenger lines then being reached by means of a double line connection. The new layout was controlled from the old signal box, which had been enlarged and now contained 96 working and 4 spare levers.

To the south of Aber Junction, on the Walnut Tree Junction branch, extensive sorting and storage sidings had

Plate 12 - A short Aber branch train waits for its engine to run round at Senghenydd, taken after the renaming of the station in 1904. Note the prominent Up Starter signal on the Down platform, installed as part of the 1901 signalling alterations to enable Up passenger trains to arrive at the Down platform.

Senghenydd

Plate 13 - A busy view of Senghenydd station at about the time of World War I, with a colliers' train stabled in the sidings to the west of the Up platform. The trailing crossover between the running lines had been added by 1915.

The Aber Branch

been provided on either side of the line. A single track ran from the Up sidings, passing to the rear of the signal box, to provide a direct link to the Aber branch.

Lt. Colonel Druitt recommended approval for the new works, subject to a number of minor requirements, in his report of 27th November 1905.

The object of the Beddau Loop was to enable traffic to and from the sidings at Aber Junction to pass directly between there and the Cardiff and Caerphilly line. The junction of this link with the Caerphilly branch at Watford Crossing was approved by Lt. Colonel Druitt on 27th June 1906.

Traffic continued to grow, however, and on 3rd January 1908 the Rhymney Board approved the provision of additional sidings at Aber Junction, cost estimated at £4,800.

Cornelius Lundie is Retired

While these alterations were proceeding an era had come to an end as far as the management of the Rhymney Railway was concerned. On 27th January 1905 the Rhymney Board had determined, clearly with some trepidation, that the time had come for their General Manager, Cornelius Lundie (then over 90 years of age) to retire.

Cornelius Lundie had been born in Kelso-on-Tweed in Roxborough in 1815 and had enjoyed a highly varied career - as resident engineer on a number of railway construction projects, estate manager, rather less than successful farmer in Ireland and Australia, and from 1855 Engineer and Manager of the Blythe and Tyne Railway - before being appointed as Traffic Manager and Engineer of the Rhymney Railway on 19th November 1861.

About 1885 he acquired the title of 'General Manager' of the company, becoming (according to his obituary in the *Proceedings of the Institution of Civil Engineers*) *'largely responsible for the policy of the company, the Directors invariably reposing complete confidence in his judgement and ability'*. Lundie was a man of strong religious beliefs, which he applied to his day-to-day affairs, being described as *'strict to severity in business matters'*, but nevertheless with a kindly side in private.

He certainly impressed E L Ahrons, who referred to him as 'a marvellous old man' who 'lived absolutely' for the Rhymney Co. By way of compensation for his enforced retirement, the Directors elected Lundie 'Consulting Director', a post he is reported to have undertaken with vigour until shortly before his death on 12th February 1908, in his 93rd year.

Such was the magnitude of the change produced by Mr Lundie's retirement that the Rhymney Board felt obliged to hold a special meeting at the Angel Hotel, Cardiff on 23rd February 1905 to consider the question of appointing a successor. It was decided to divide Lundie's domain, like Gaul, into three parts, with Ernest Prosser, the old man's deputy, becoming Manager (but on his existing salary), W J Griffiths, Engineer, and R Jenkins, Locomotive Engineer. This triumvirate did not last long, however, for on 2nd

(Right) Figure 11 - Aber Junction as depicted by a 1915 OS map. The map, of course, shows the considerable changes of 1904/1905.

In evidence are the four tracks southwards from Pwllypant and extensive sidings and junctions. The rail installations here took the form of a large X; Aber Junction itself is at the foot of the plan whilst a few chains to the south is Walnut Tree Junction, where the lines to Caerphilly and Taffs Well diverge.

The Barry Company's Penyrheol Viaduct crosses the very end of Aber Junction Sidings.

March 1906 Prosser was elevated to the position of General Manager of the Rhymney Co., his salary being increased from £750 to £1,000 a year in the process.

Prosser, a native of Cardiff, had joined the company as a junior clerk in 1881 and had risen through the ranks to the position of Deputy General Manager, a post he had held for the last five years of Lundie's reign. He was to prove an efficient and forward looking chief officer for the Rhymney Railway for the rest of its independent existence.

Following the introduction of steam railcars between Caerphilly and Senghenydd on 1st October 1907 *(see Chapter Five)*, the Rhymney Board agreed, at its meeting on 1st November, to the expenditure of £260 on the erection of a halt at Aber Junction, to be served by these vehicles. The provisional sanction of the Board of Trade for 'Beddau Halt' was granted on 25th March 1908, enabling its opening to take place on 1st April. The new halt was situated on the main line to Caerphilly, about a quarter of a mile south-east of Aber Junction.

Lt. Colonel Druitt completed his report of inspection of Beddau Halt for the Board of Trade on 9th April, noting that Up and Down platforms, each 130ft long, had been constructed of old sleepers and appeared to be 'rather rough'. They were linked by ramps to the public road, which passed under the railway just north of the halt, but lacked any form of shelter. Druitt was satisfied with the arrangements and recommended approval, provided the halt was used only by the steam railcars.

At Caerphilly station the cars arrived at the Down platform, then reversed by means of a crossover to the east of the station, to depart from the Up side. To enable the car to stand clear of the running lines between trips, a short trailing siding was provided off the Up line, immediately to the east of the Up platform. This was approved by the Rhymney Board on 3rd January 1908, at an estimated cost of £350, and was reported to be ready for inspection on 25th February. Board of Trade approval was recommended by Lt. Colonel Druitt on 9th April.

By this date the facilities at Caerphilly were clearly inadequate in relation to the needs of the traffic. There were only two lines through the station, with platforms on each. The main station buildings were on the Down side, with the goods yard alongside. In addition to the Aber

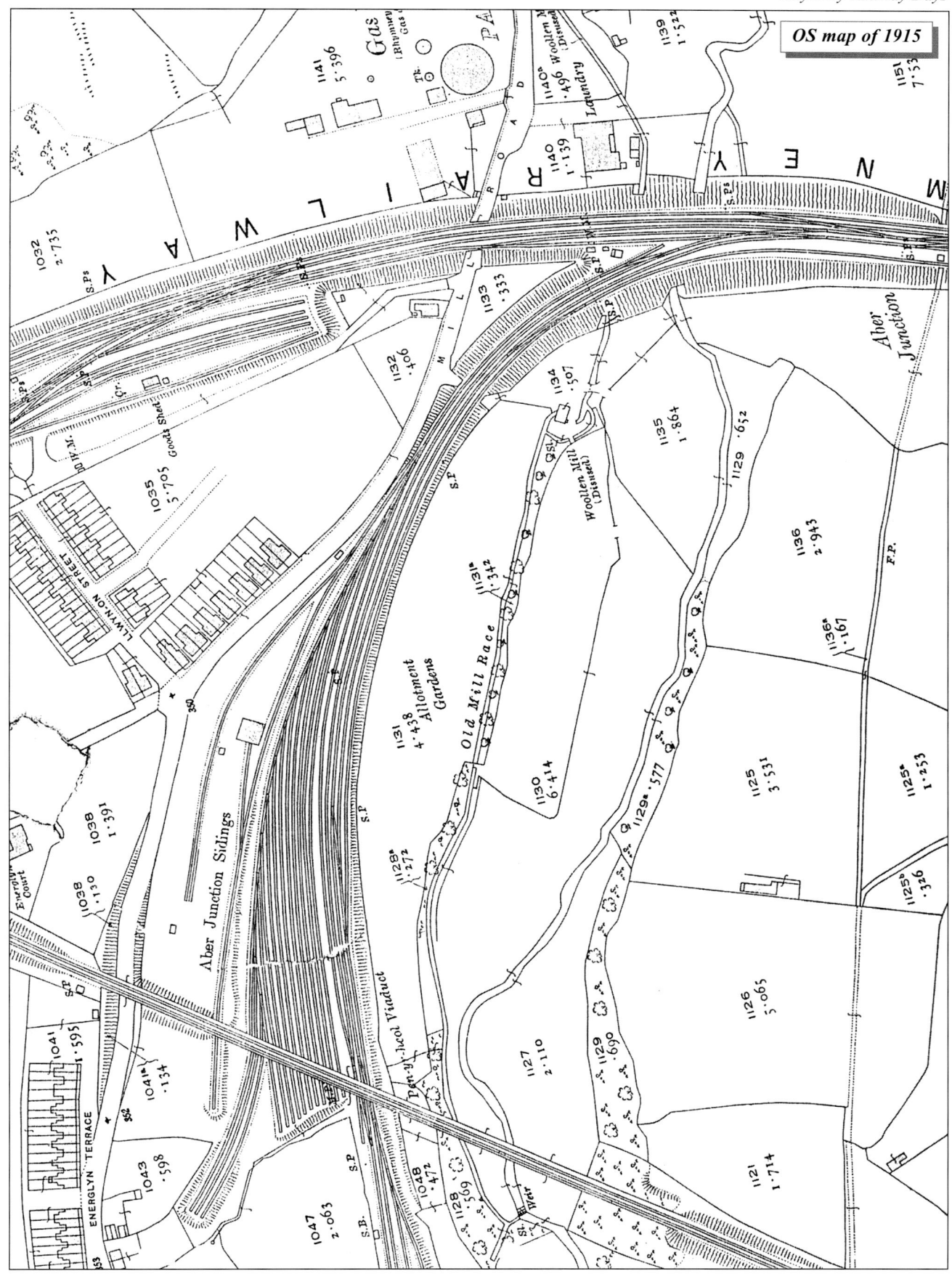

Rhymney Railway Days

OS map of 1915

The Aber Branch

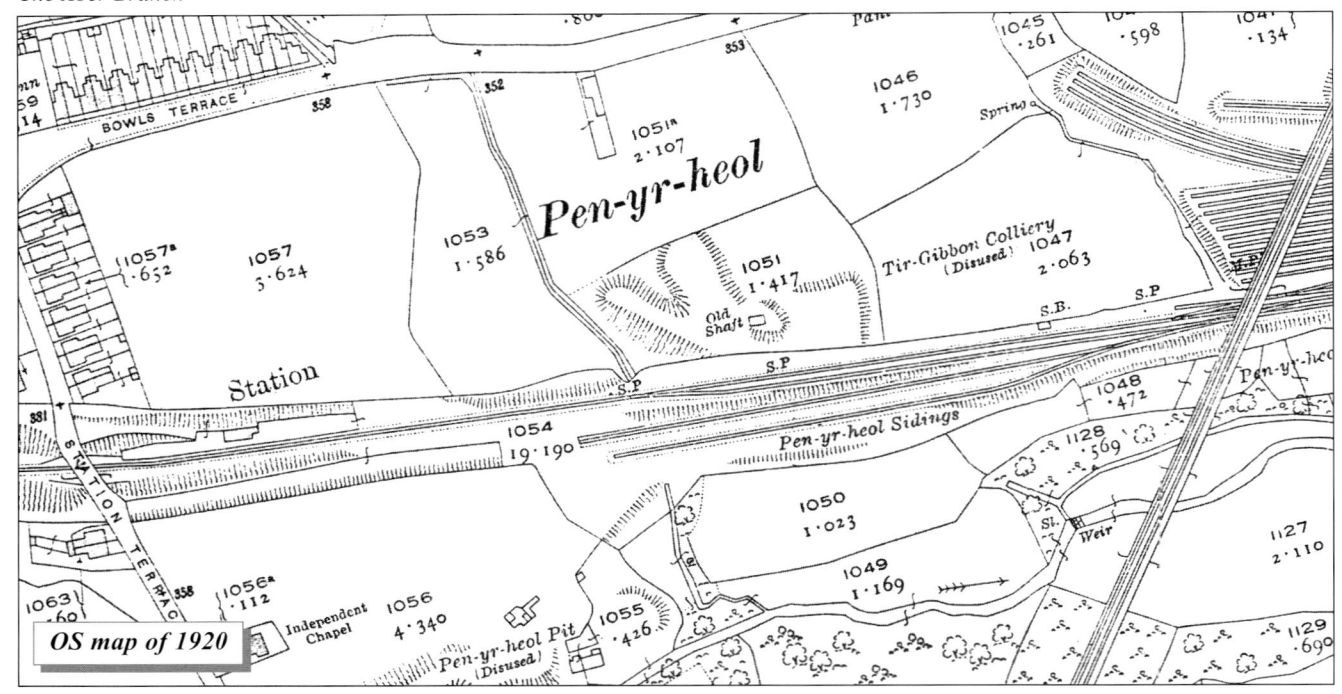

OS map of 1920

Valley motor cars, the station was also used by the main Rhymney Railway service between Cardiff and Rhymney and Merthyr, GWR trains between Pontypridd and Newport and a steam railcar service operated by the Alexandra (Newport and South Wales) Docks and Railway (AD&R) from Pontypridd (Tram Road) station. These services shared the lines through the station with the expanding mineral traffic, made up of Rhymney trains passing to and from Cardiff and AD&R workings between Pontypridd and Newport. The growing volume of traffic, combined with the limited facilities, led to serious and worsening congestion at the station.

Another complication was the prospect of the Barry Co. bringing an additional passenger service into the station. Under its Act of 1896 that company's Rhymney branch, between Tynycaeau and Penrhos Junctions, was required to be laid out as a passenger railway. A passenger service to Caerphilly was to be introduced should the Board of Trade decide, following an application from Glamorgan County Council, that this was in the public interest. This provision had been a significant coup for the County Council, which had sought, as a matter of policy, to ensure that passenger trains were run on what would otherwise have been freight-only lines.

Excursion traffic from the Rhymney Valley and beyond destined for Barry Island, via the Rhymney branch of the ByR, commenced in the Summer of 1902. This, the Barry Co. felt, satisfied the real demand on the route, whereas a regular timetabled service, as sought by the County Council, was likely to prove unremunerative. In November 1904 the railway company suggested that a railcar service be provided to Pwllypant on its B&MR extension, thereby avoiding the need to make use of Caerphilly station. This idea was not taken any further, but on 10th March 1908 an

(Above) Figure 12 - The station and sidings at Penyrheol. The remains of the early collieries area apparent, Aber Junction Sidings are encroaching and the Barry Railway's viaduct straddles all.

(Below) Plate 14 - Penyrheol signal box in Rhymney days. At its inspection in 1893 this box contained 18 working and 4 spare levers.

24

Plate 15 - Caerphilly station prior to the great rebuilding, looking towards Senghenydd.

agreement was concluded with the Rhymney Co., whereby the ByR would contribute towards the cost of enlarging that station. 8The following June the Barry General Manager suggested that a passenger service should put on between Tynycaeau Junction (where connections would be made with trains on the Barry main line) and Caerphilly, but again no further progress was apparent.

Caerphilly Rebuilding

Improvement of the passenger accommodation at Caerphilly required the removal of the adjoining goods yard, and its replacement on a new site. Plans for the new facility were approved by the Rhymney Board on 2nd October 1908, the location being about a mile to the east of the old one, sandwiched between the Rhymney main line and the branch to Machen. Land assembly and other preliminaries took some time to complete and it was not until 10th February 1910 that the tender of Marnes Chaplin & Co. was accepted for the earthworks and masonry (at £12,605 5s 5d).

The re-siting of the goods station met with strong disapproval from local tradesmen, hauliers and other users. A public meeting, held at Caerphilly on 3rd October 1911, heard numerous complaints about the inconvenience and additional cost resulting from the increased distance of the goods facilities from the town centre. A deputation was appointed to take these views to the Rhymney Board, but there was no going back. On 8th February 1912 the Directors agreed to proceed with the reconstruction of the passenger station, taking in land previously occupied by the old goods yard.

This work proceeded apace, despite the scale and complexity of the undertaking, and on 23rd October 1914 the Board of Trade was advised that the arrangements were complete and that the new station was ready for inspection. As was by now almost customary, Lt. Colonel Druitt presided over this event, his report of 25th November stating:

'I have the honour to report for the information of the Board of Trade, that in compliance with the instructions contained in your Minute of 27th October, I have inspected the new station at Caerphilly, on the Rhymney Railway.

At this place two additional lines have been constructed through the station, which has been entirely rebuilt. There are three platforms accommodating five platform lines, viz. No.1 Up platform, 800 feet long, 20 feet wide, 3 feet above rail level; Platform No.2: an island platform for Nos.2 and 3 platform lines, 800 feet long, 30 feet wide and 3 feet above rail level; Platform No.3: 600 feet long, 20 feet wide and 3 feet above rail level, for No.4 through line and No.5 bay line.

A new overhead booking office and large waiting room have been provided alongside the public road overbridge adjoining. No.1 platform is approached by a ramp, and the two island platforms by flights of stairs. On the first two platforms very good accommodation and conveniences for both sexes have been provided; on the third there are conveniences for men only, and no waiting room etc. Luggage lifts have been provided for Nos.2 and 3 platforms.'

Lt. Colonel Druitt found these arrangements to be satisfactory and recommended that the final approval of

The Aber Branch

Plate 16 - Caerphilly station with a Rhymney Railway 0-6-2T shunting a single wagon alongside Platform No.3. The booking office, which spanned all four lines and their platforms, is visible beyond the engine.

the Board of Trade be granted.

The revised layout in the vicinity of the station commenced at a complex set of junctions at Caerphilly West Junction, where the Caerphilly branch joined the main line from Aber Junction, all controlled by a new signal box, containing 52 working and 4 spare levers. From this point two sets of double lines ran through the station to another set of junctions at Caerphilly East Junction, where the new signal box was provided with 111 working and 21 spare levers. These arrangements had already been approved by Lt. Colonel Druitt during an earlier inspection, reported on 19th December 1913.

The Rhymney Directors were informed, at their meeting on 4th December 1914, that Board of Trade sanction for the new station had been granted. Accordingly, it was agreed to send to the ByR Co. an account for £8,000, this sum being considered to represent that company's contribution to the cost of the station reconstruction. However, the Barry Board took the view that as the plans for the new station had not been approved by its own Engineer (on the grounds that the facilities proposed were not appropriate to his company's needs) it did not wish to part with this amount of money. When the required payment was not forthcoming the Rhymney Co. took the matter to the High Court, where the two companies agreed, in 1917, to suspend further consideration of this issue until after the war. In the event, changed circumstances following the return of peace meant that the question remained unresolved until rendered immaterial by the amalgamation of the two concerns with the GWR in 1922.

Modernisation on a somewhat smaller scale was foreshadowed on 7th February 1913 when the Rhymney Board approved the replacement of the oil lamps at Abertridwr and Senghenydd stations with gas lighting.

The Barry Co.'s reluctance to extend its passenger operations to Caerphilly did not apply in the case of freight traffic, as on 20th December 1912 its Directors agreed to open a goods station for the Caerphilly district adjoining the Energlyn Sidings on the company's B&MR extension. The new depot, which the ByR named 'Caerphilly', was opened on 18th August 1913 and was situated at the southern end of the sidings, about a quarter of a mile from Penyrheol station.

The output of the Aber Valley collieries, in common

(Right) Figure 13 - A diagram of lines around Caerphilly to consolidate the position at 1922. As well as the diversity of routes converging on the junctions at Penrhos, the changes discussed so far are evident on the plan - the new junctions at Caerphilly, the Barry Railway's incursion and connection at Energlyn, the Rhymney Company's Beddau Loop and Beddau Halt.

Rhymney Railway Days

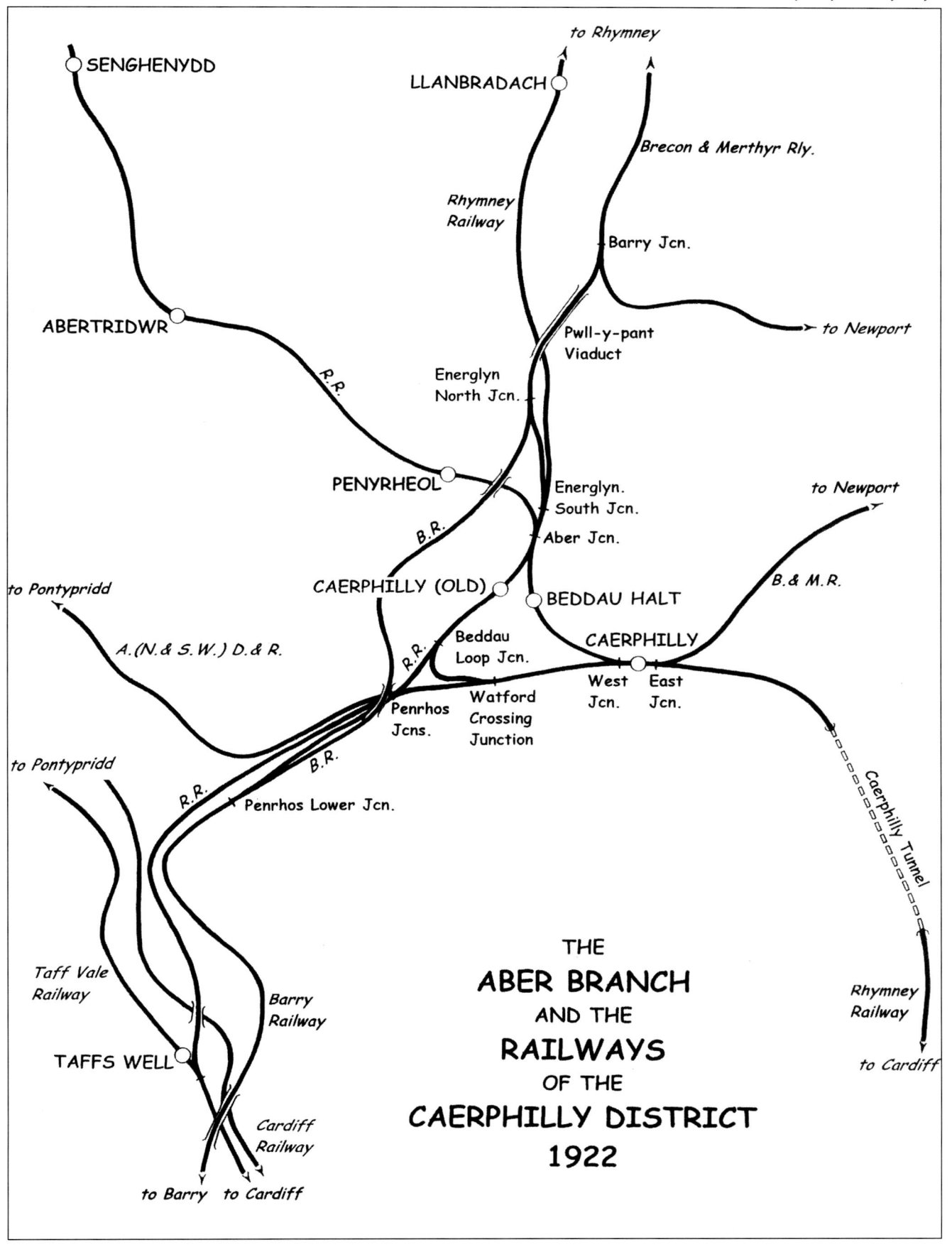

THE
ABER BRANCH
AND THE
RAILWAYS
OF THE
CAERPHILLY DISTRICT
1922

27

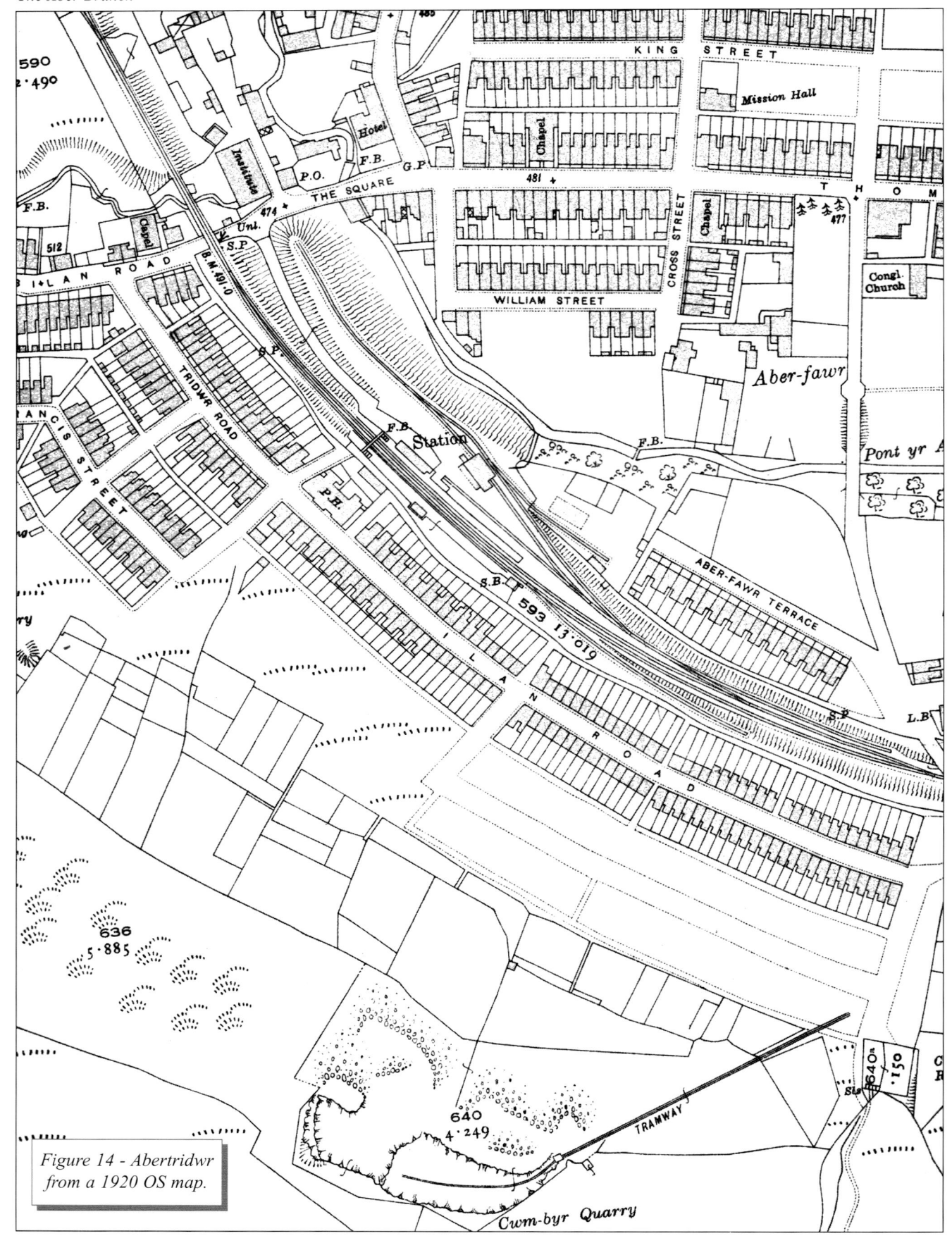

The Aber Branch

Figure 14 - Abertridwr from a 1920 OS map.

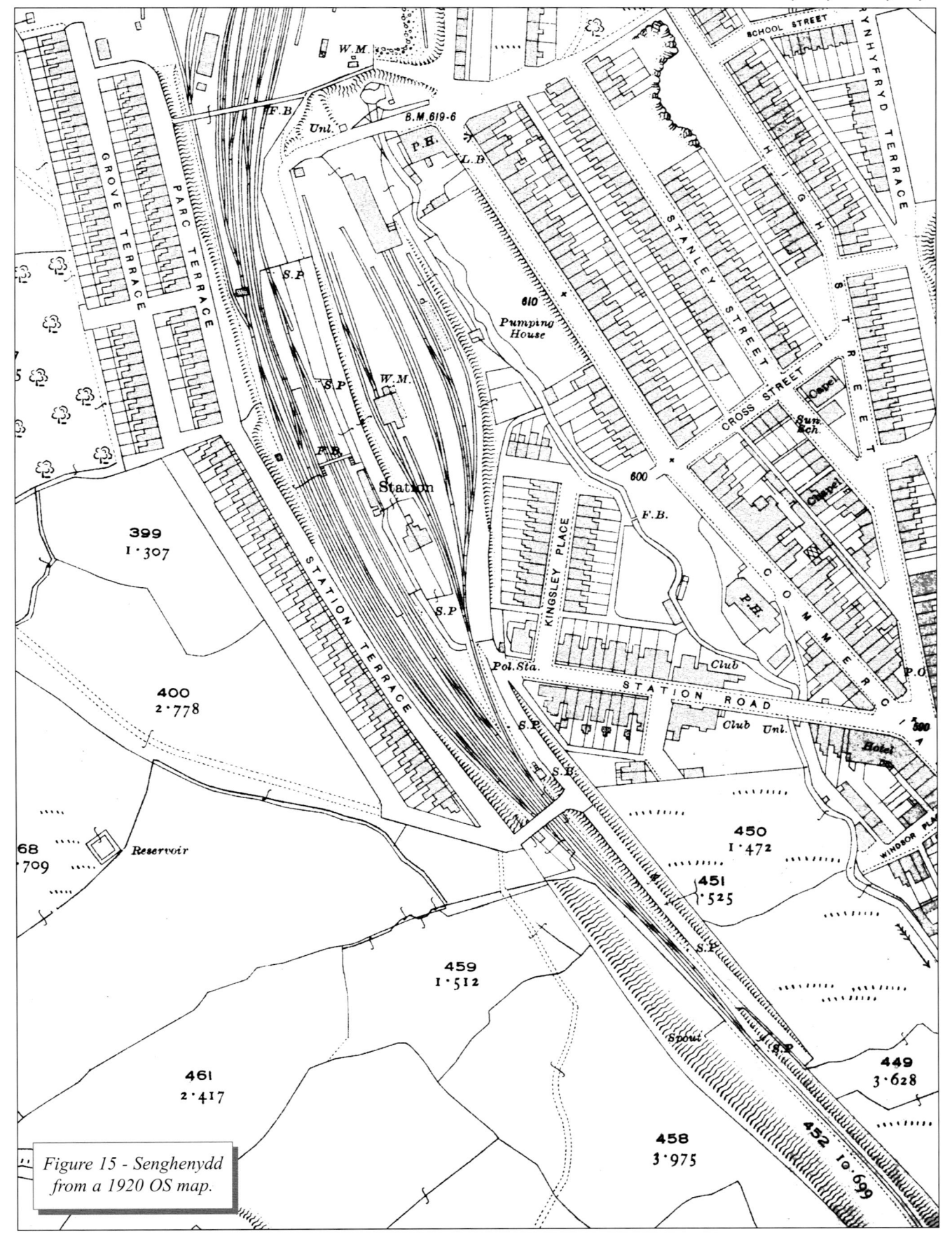

Figure 15 - Senghenydd from a 1920 OS map.

The Aber Branch

Plate 23 - The ghostly remains of Universal Colliery, Senghenydd on 12th May 1952.

Prior to the end of coal production at Universal Colliery, authorisation had been given for a number of alterations to the track and signalling arrangements associated with the colliery sidings at Senghenydd. These were inspected by Lt. Colonel A H L Mount, on behalf of the Minister of Transport, on 7th November 1928, and consisted of a facing connection from the Up line to the colliery sidings adjoining the Up platform, in place of the earlier trailing connection to the Down line. An Up home signal, equipped with a route indicator, and a Down advanced starting signal had also been provided. As coal production had ceased by the date of the inspection, it is not clear as to what, if any, use was made of these new facilities.

Changes and rationalisation

The railways of South Wales also saw a substantial decline in local goods traffic, much of which was over comparatively short distances and highly vulnerable to competition from road transport. The GWR attempted to stem the tide by the introduction of the Railhead Distribution system of motor lorries based on major goods depots. While this initiative retained traffic for the company, it often did so at the expense of railborne goods to local stations. The Cardiff network included a run from Caerphilly up the Aber Valley to Abertridwr and Senghenydd.

The Grouping also provided the opportunity for the implementation of various rationalisation and improvement schemes in South Wales. One of the most significant of these involved the closure of the former ByR extension to the B&MR, which, under unified ownership, was soon deemed to be redundant. Abandonment of this line was sanctioned by the GWR Act of 4th August 1926. However, it was not until 1937 that removal of the girders of Penyrheol Viaduct took place. The main spans, each of which weighed 35 tons, proved too unwieldy to lift, and so were pushed off the tops of the piers into the valley below. They were then cut up and the pieces loaded into railway wagons using a crane that was standing on the remaining part of the viaduct.

A similar procedure was employed later that year when the larger Llanbradach Viaduct was demolished, although in this case the recovered steel was conveyed by lorry to Caerphilly and Llanbradach stations for despatch by rail. Two features that survived this retrenchment were the former ByR sidings and goods station at Energlyn, the latter continuing in use until 1960.

In May 1923 it had been announced that the GWR intended to construct a new spur between the Cardiff and Caerphilly line and the ex TVR Roath branch where the two lines crossed near Roath. In the event, this link, which had earlier featured in abortive Cardiff Railway proposals, was not proceeded with. Instead, it was found more appropriate to work coal traffic from the former Rhymney Railway system, bound for Cardiff Docks, via Walnut Tree Junction and the ex TVR lines. As a result, traffic from Aber Junction was routed away from the Beddau Loop onto the single line section between Penrhos Junction and Walnut Tree

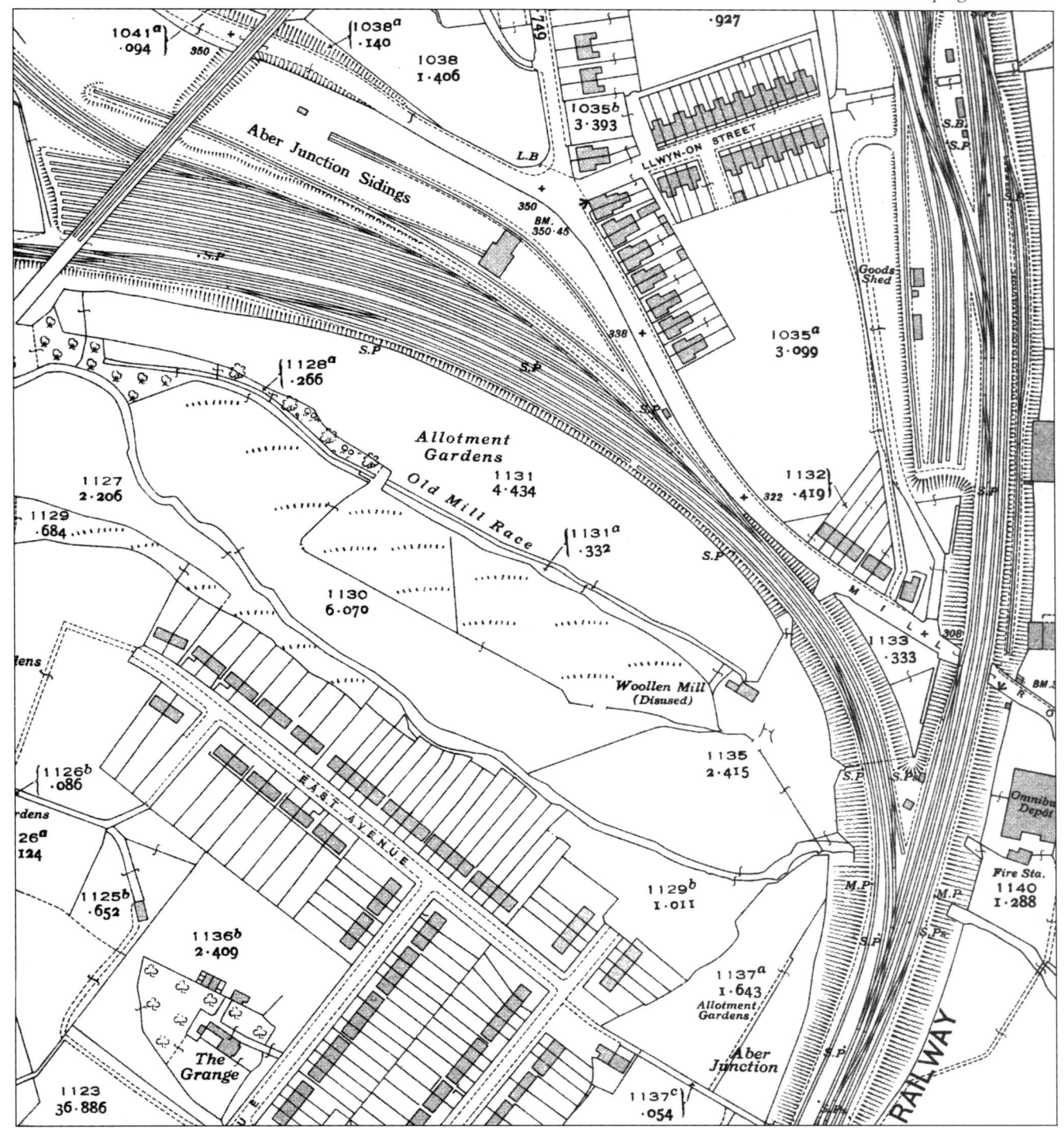

Figure 18 - Aber Junction, Aber Junction Sidings and Energlyn goods depot. The plan shows that some of the track has been removed from Penyrheol Viaduct on the closed ex Barry Railway line; 1937 OS map.

Junction. To avoid congestion and delay a second track was brought into use here on 12th February 1928.

Rhymney line passenger trains had always been handicapped by the layout of the railway at the Cardiff end, which prevented direct access from the Parade station to Bute Road (serving the docks and associated commercial sector) and Cardiff General stations. Consequently, any passengers wishing to continue their journeys to these destinations were forced to transfer either to the nearby Queen Street station or to the electric tramway. As part of a comprehensive scheme aimed, in part, at facilitating through working, Parade station was closed from 15th April 1928, Rhymney line trains running instead into Queen Street station.

The Aber Branch

The inter-war period also saw the installation of a number of sand drags on various steeply graded sections throughout South Wales. One such location was at Abertridwr station, where Down trains had to negotiate a descent of 1 in 51. The completed drag, which had been authorised by the GWR on 31st March 1927, was inspected and approved by Lt. Colonel A H L Mount, on behalf of the Minister of Transport, on 7th November 1928. The new works comprised a facing connection off the Down line of the passing loop, leading to the drag itself, which was 125ft long.

Government assistance and war

To provide relief from the extreme levels of unemployment in depressed areas such as the South Wales valleys, the Government of the day promoted the Development (Loan Guarantees and Grants) Act of 1929. This enabled the GWR to carry out various improvements which otherwise would not have been commercially viable. In particular, a number of new engine sheds were constructed to replace certain inadequate or obsolete facilities of pre-Grouping origin.

The former Rhymney Railway shed at Senghenydd was not well placed to deal with the changed patterns of working which had come into being following the grouping of 1922. Traffic on the Senghenydd branch itself had declined and the location of the shed at the branch terminus produced a substantial number of light engine movements to and from the sidings at Aber Junction. It was therefore decided to close the shed and transfer its locomotive allocation elsewhere. At the same time, a proposal was developed to replace the small ex TVR shed at Radyr with a much larger one, capable of accommodating twenty four engines compared with the previous six.

The new shed at Radyr was brought into use in 1931, following the demise of the old one on 29th March of that year. Closure of Senghenydd shed took place on 23rd May. Over 40 men had been employed in the locomotive department at Senghenydd and at closure these were redeployed, seven going to Swindon, six to Aberdare, five to Radyr, four to Rhymney, three to Westbury, two each to Treherbert, Weymouth and Yeovil, and one each to Barry, Bristol, Pontypridd Coke Ovens, Goodwick, Hengoed, Old Oak Common, Reading, Severn Tunnel Junction, Stourbridge and Trowbridge. However, although the closure did not result in a direct increase in unemployment in the area, the loss of spending power represented yet another blow to the economic vitality of the Aber Valley in the wake of the end of coal production at Universal Colliery some three years earlier.

With the declaration of war on 3rd September 1939 Government control of the national railway system was re-established through the Railway Executive Committee. Additional powers to such effect had been obtained under the Emergency Powers Defence Act 1939, while the

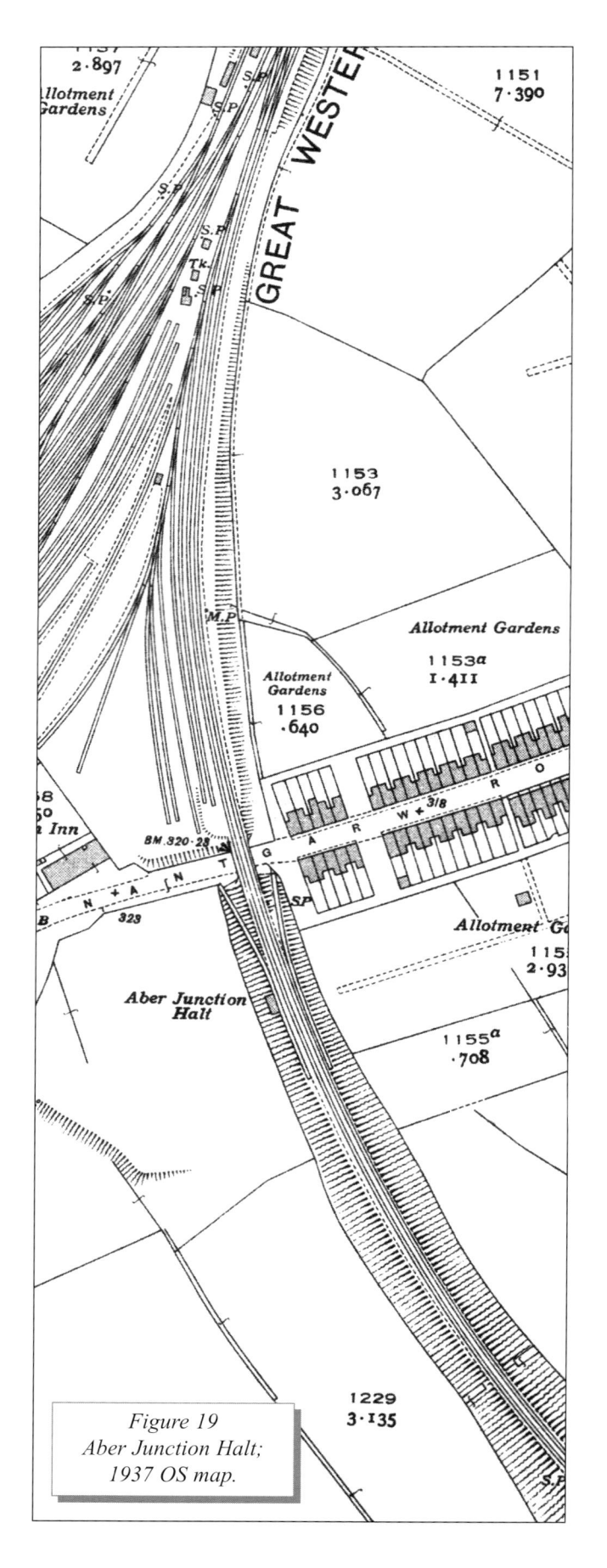

*Figure 19
Aber Junction Halt;
1937 OS map.*

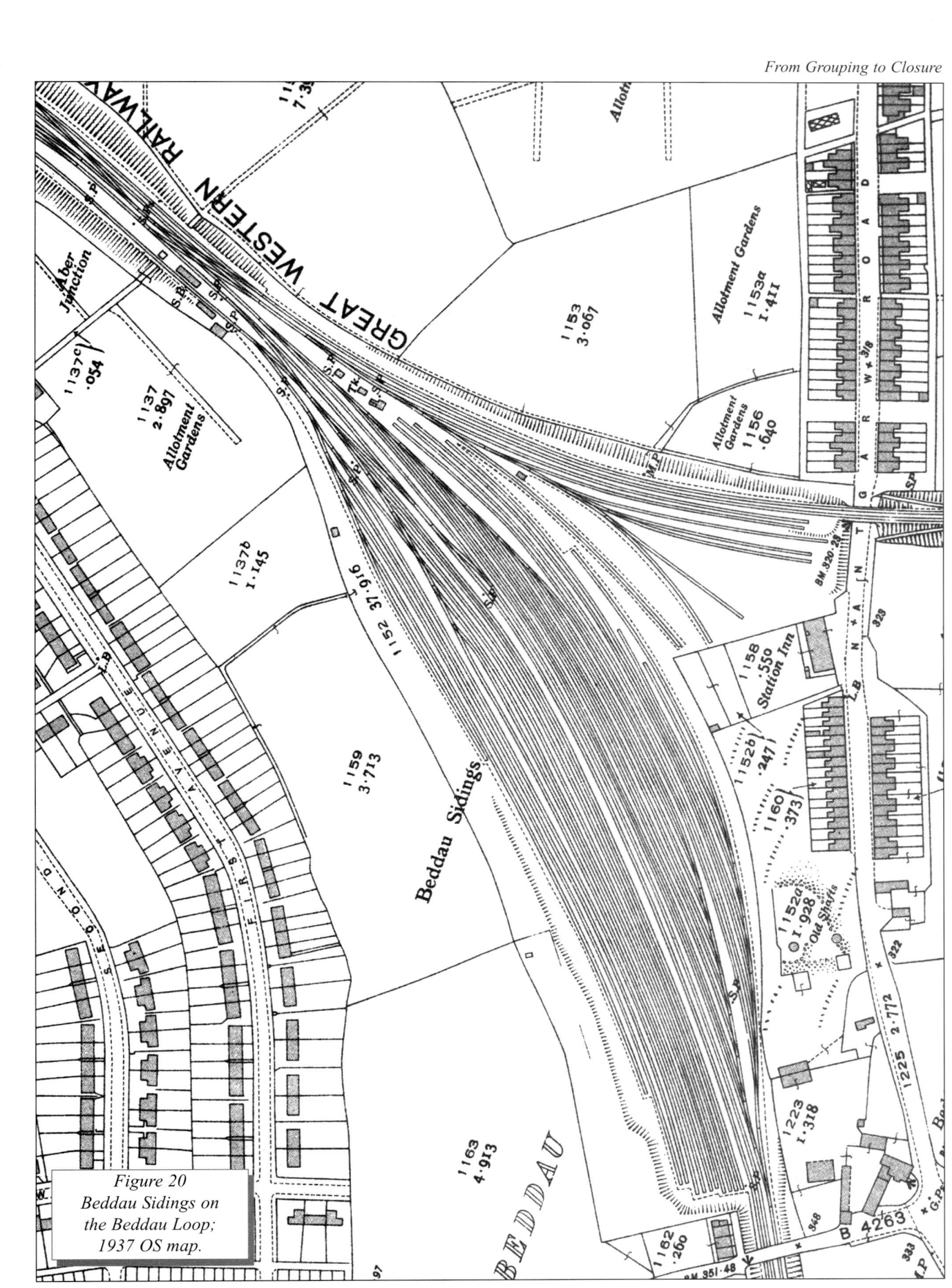

*Figure 20
Beddau Sidings on
the Beddau Loop;
1937 OS map.*

railway system was, of course, much less fragmented than had been the case in 1914. Passenger train services generally were reduced in frequency and decelerated but, unlike World War I, this occurred against the backdrop of heavy restrictions on private motoring as a result of petrol rationing, together with greatly curtailed bus timetables. The result, despite attempts to discourage travel (as exemplified by the 'Is your journey really necessary?' campaign), was a substantial increase in passenger traffic. Not surprisingly, given these circumstances, the Aber branch trains also experienced an upturn in patronage.

The war years also saw a further decline in the fortunes of the export coal trade of South Wales, especially after the fall of France in June 1940. As a result, the colliery companies pressed for their output to be redirected to inland markets, but this was resisted by the GWR fearful of the increased congestion that could result on key wartime routes. When this opposition was overcome coal movements to inland destinations grew significantly, and by April 1941 this traffic was up 20 per cent on the 1939 figure.

One development affecting the Senghenydd branch during this period was the construction of a new colliers' platform to serve Windsor Colliery. This was provided under an agreement with Powell Duffryn Associated Collieries, dated 4th October 1943 (*see Chapter Six for details*), and was on the site of an earlier and probably less substantial structure.

The return of peace saw the nation's railways in an even worse condition than had been the case in 1918. The undoubted contribution made to the war effort had left the system in a very run down state, with substantial arrears in maintenance and new construction. National shortages also continued to make their impact, while it did not take long for road transport to make good the depredations of the war years and to resume its upward path.

Post-war and Nationalisation

This desperate situation was compounded by the severe winter of 1946/47, especially in South Wales. A blizzard of extreme proportions struck on 4th March 1947, severing communications with over 200 mines, including Windsor Colliery in the Aber Valley. The resulting coal supply crisis led directly to a substantial reduction in the GWR's Passenger Service Timetable for the following summer.

The year 1947 saw the authorisation of the last significant new investment in our area of study prior to Nationalisation, when the GWR ordered the building of a new signal box and other alterations at Aber Junction. These were not inspected until 5th May 1953 when they were approved by Brigadier Langley. In addition to the new signal box the opportunity had been taken to alter the position of certain signals and to provide track circuits. Energlyn signal box had been closed, its former connections now being power operated and controlled from Aber Junction signal box.

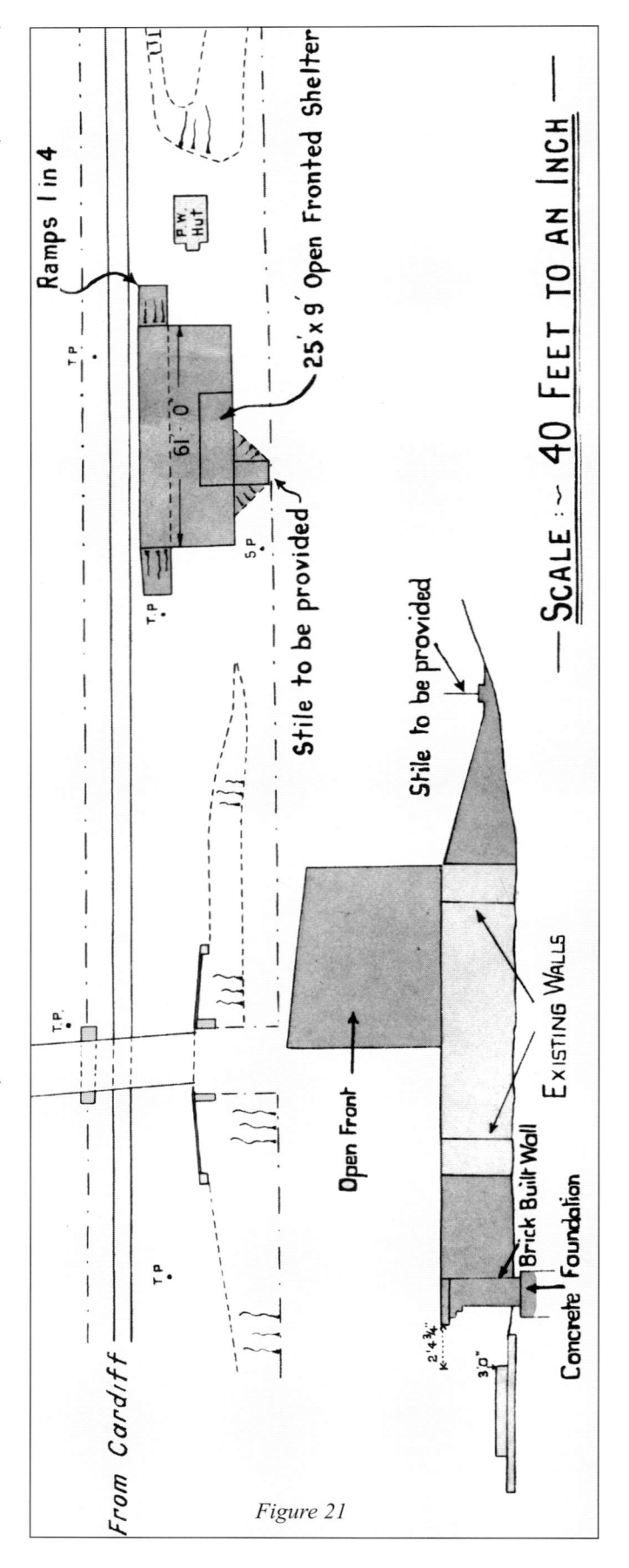

Figure 21

From Grouping to Closure

(Above) Plate 24 - Windsor Colliery and its colliers' platform, looking towards Abertridwr on 11th June 1964.

(Left) Figure 21 - This drawing of the Windsor Colliery colliers' platform was titled 'Abertridwr Halt'.

(Below) Plate 25 - The view at Penyrheol towards Senghenydd on 11th June 1962. The overbridge had been built, somewhat optimistically, to accommodate double track.

The Aber Branch

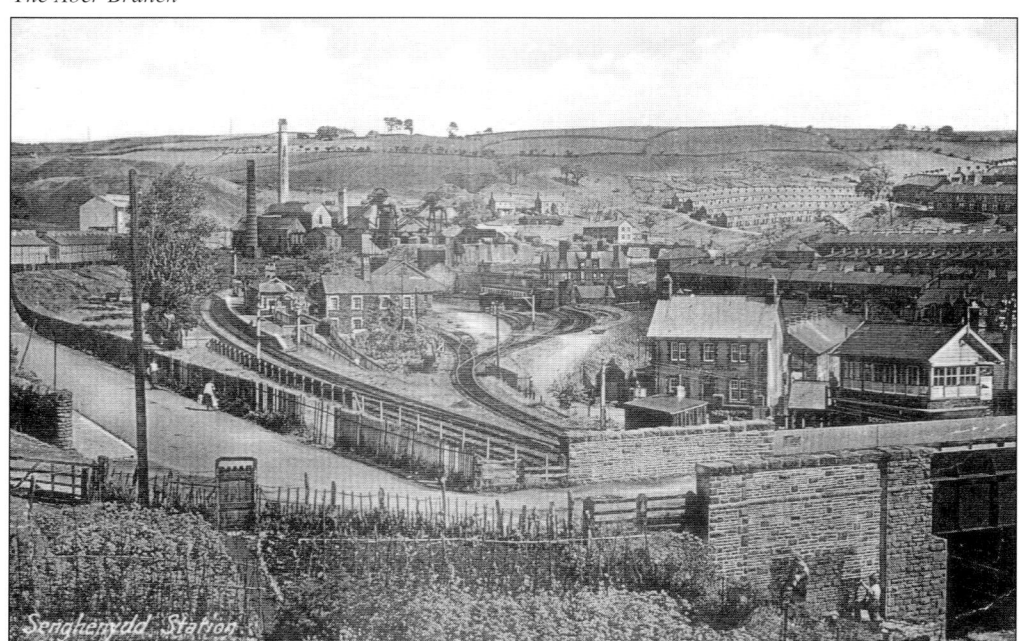

Plate 26 - A postcard of Senghenydd post-1933 after the engine shed had been demolished. The coal sidings behind the Up platform have also gone. Note that pointing of the bridge brickwork seems to be in progress.

The election of a Labour Government in 1945 had brought nationalisation to the fore as the panacea for the problems facing the nation's railways. This proposal was given effect under the Transport Act of 6th August 1947 and, from 1st January 1948, the GWR gave way to Western Region of British Railways.

It will be recalled that Penyrheol station had been downgraded to halt status in 1930. However, it was not until the start of the summer service on 8th June 1953 that this change in designation was acknowledged in the public timetable. Even then, the station nameboard continued to proclaim 'Penyrheol' only until the end of the passenger service. The station building remained in place and in other use despite this change.

Closure of the nearby goods yard followed on 16th July 1957, but the signal box continued in use, principally to control the transition from double to single line, which occurred just before Penyrheol Halt was reached.

New housing and factory development in the vicinity of Aber Junction Halt had placed an increasing strain on its primitive facilities, largely unaltered since Rhymney Railway days. On 15th October 1954 major alterations were approved to make the amenities at the Halt more appropriate to the volume of traffic then being handled. The platforms were reconstructed and lengthened using pre-cast concrete units manufactured at the Regional Concrete Depot in Taunton. Two corrugated iron waiting shelters were provided, together with a booking hut at the north end of the Down platform. The new works were inspected by Lt. Colonel Wilson, representing the Minister of Transport and Civil Aviation, on 21st September 1955. His report noted that 4,000-4,500 passengers per week were being booked at the halt. It was especially busy in mornings and afternoons as it was used by pupils attending the nearby Caerphilly Girls' Grammar School.

The future of the Senghenydd branch must have seemed more secure when diesel multiple units (dmus) first appeared in 1958. Operations continued much as they had done in the days of steam, and there was no immediate curtailment of track layouts or signalling as a result of this change. However, the closure of the goods yard at Senghenydd on 2nd July 1962 removed the need for the run round loop and sidings at the station. The signal box at the branch terminus was closed on 17th February 1963.

Increasing closures

The late 1950s and early 1960s was a period of 'piecemeal' closures, resulting in the gradual elimination of many branch line passenger services in South Wales. While the Senghenydd branch had remained busier than some of these lines, the unrelenting nature of this closure process pointed to a very uncertain future. It cannot have come as a great surprise to those with an interest in the branch, therefore, when Caerphilly to Senghenydd appeared in the schedule of passenger services to be withdrawn appended to the Beeching Report, published on 27th March 1963. Of the branch line services in South Wales only those which ran through to Cardiff were deemed sufficiently important to escape the axe, the contribution of 'feeder' services, such as that of the Aber Valley, to the main routes being given little weight.

The Western Region lost little time in publishing the formal notice for the closure proposal, which appeared in June 1963. This stated that unless objections were received the Caerphilly to Senghenydd passenger service would be withdrawn on 9th September. This announcement was met with considerable local opposition, leading to the formation of the Aber Valley Anti Railway Closure Committee. The closure proposal then became one of six (the others being Cardiff to Coryton, Abercynon to

Plate 27 - Class '37' Co-Co No.37 282 leaves the Up side yard past Aber Junction signal box with a trip working from Radyr Yard to Bargoed Pits on 3rd April 1978.

Aberdare, Porth to Maerdy, Barry to Bridgend and Cardiff (General) to Cardiff (Clarence Road)) considered by the Transport Users Consultative Committee for Wales and Monmouthshire (TUCC) at a hearing which took place in Cardiff commencing 26th August 1963. The TUCC subsequently accepted the case, as put forward by British Railways, for the closure to passengers of all of the lines under threat, with the exception of that between Cardiff and Coryton, which was reprieved and continues in operation to this day. The withdrawal of the Caerphilly to Senghenydd service was confirmed by the Minister of Transport, Ernest Marples, in a statement made public on 17th January 1964. The Minister's approval was subject to the running of additional early morning and late evening buses on the route parallel to the railway.

The date for the withdrawal of the passenger service was fixed for Monday, 15th June 1964, but as there was no Sunday service, the last train ran on Saturday, 13th June. The trains themselves were crowded, but there was a sense of bitterness in the realisation that something worthwhile was about to be taken away. The last Up train from Caerphilly at 6.53pm conveyed local councillors and a large party of pupils from the Groeswen Secondary School, together with railway enthusiasts and local people. On arrival at the branch terminus a banner was unfurled displaying the name of the school and the date and time of the last train. The final departure from Senghenydd at 7.17pm was accompanied by a fusillade of fog signals, which echoed across the valley, and cheers from the attendant crowd. The three-car dmu then made its way back down the valley over track that was, in many places, in poor condition, its speed rarely exceeding 20mph.

Monday, 15th June 1964 was indeed a black day for the railways of South Wales, with no less than six passenger train services, including that of the Senghenydd branch, being withdrawn. The others were Barry to Bridgend, Dowlais to Nelson & Llancaiach, Neath to Pontypool Road, Porth to Maerdy and Swansea (Victoria) to Pontadulais. Two other local services - Abercynon to Aberdare and Cardiff (General) to Cardiff (Clarence Road) - had already gone on 16th March of that year.

With the end of the passenger service the line from just beyond Windsor Colliery North Ground Frame was closed to all traffic. On the remainder of the branch very little time was lost in carrying out certain alterations that reflected its changed status. Sunday, 14th June 1964 had seen the closure of the signal boxes at Penyrheol and Abertridwr and the conversion of the line to one engine in steam operation, sufficient to cater for the Windsor Colliery coal traffic and the small amount of goods still handled at Abertridwr yard. The latter did not survive for long, however, its closure taking place on 1st March 1965.

The publication of the Beeching Report, with the threat it posed for the future of the Senghenydd branch, coincided with the removal of another reminder of the valley's past. During March 1963 officers and men of the 100 Squadron

The Aber Branch

Plate 28 - The bitter end; the end of the line at Senghenydd in 1963 after singling.

Royal Engineers (Monmouthshire Militia) blew up the old engine house and other derelict buildings at Universal Colliery. The pithead winding gear was dismantled and the site then levelled for development. However, it was not until the summer of 1979 that the two shafts were finally filled and capped with concrete.

The surviving section of the Senghenydd branch continued in use for the transport of coal from Windsor Colliery for another 12 years after the withdrawal of the passenger trains in 1964. Work started in 1974 to link the colliery workings with those of the nearby Nantgarw Colliery, in the Taff Valley, thereby enabling Windsor coal to be brought to the surface at that mine. The last coal trains were worked from Windsor Colliery on 4th December 1976, the colliery's output then being transferred to Nantgarw. The branch itself was finally closed on 5th September 1977, with the exception of short sections of track at Aber Junction, which were retained as sidings until 18th October 1981. Aber Junction signal box was closed on 2nd May 1987, by which time its condition was causing some concern.

Coal continued to be raised at Nantgarw for another ten years, the last trains being loaded on 21st November 1987. However, it was not until 19th November 1990 that the branch line to the colliery site was finally taken out of use.

The Beddau Loop, together with the Penrhos Junction to Caerphilly West Junction section, had been closed on 1st May 1967. From Aber Junction coal trains continued to be worked down the 'Big Hill' to Walnut Tree Junction, but from 21st June 1982 the remaining traffic was transferred, on an 'experimental' basis, to the Cardiff and Caerphilly line, via Cardiff Queen Street. This routing soon became permanent and the Aber Junction to Walnut Tree Junction line remained closed, its track being removed in the Spring of 1984.

Aber Junction Halt, which had remained open for Cardiff to Rhymney trains, was renamed 'Aber Halt', with effect from 6th May 1968. The suffix 'Halt' was deleted, as part of a national policy change, from 5th May 1969.

Although not located on the branch itself, the continued survival of Aber station maintains a physical presence for the passenger railway at the mouth of the Aber Valley and is a reminder of those increasingly far off days when it was the first stop for auto-trains, bound for Senghenydd, after leaving Caerphilly station.

Figure 22 - A luggage label of the Rhymney Railway era.

70

Rhymney Railway.

PENYRHEOL.

44

Plate 29 - A general view of the station in pre-grouping days, looking towards Senghenydd.

Abertridwr

Plate 30 - A similar view towards Senghenydd on 2nd September 1957. The Windsor Colliery spoil tips are more prominent than in the pre-grouping picture and the large private warehouse to the rear of the Up platform has been demolished.

The Aber Branch

Plate 31 - Class '64XX' No.6436 at Senghenydd, the date on the photograph c.1948. Note that the Starter signal at the Down end of the Up platform is still in situ. The signal was scheduled to be taken out of use on 28th May 1947 (see Figure 34, page 80) but that does not, of course, mean that the signal would have been removed at that time. Alternatively, the photograph might be slightly earlier than the caption suggests.

Changing Times

Plate 32 - Class '64XX' No.6402 with a two-coach auto-train at Senghenydd on 2nd September 1957. Both the bridge and signal have gone and the carriage stock has been updated, the Cardiff Railway trailers having been withdrawn by 1957.

Plate 33 - The final indignity! A platform seat is manhandled into the guard's van at Abertridwr on the final day of service, 13th June 1964.

Plate 34 - A three-car dmu leaving Penyrheol on 31st May 1962.

5
Locomotive and Train Working

The introduction of a passenger train service on the Aber branch could not be accommodated from within the existing coaching stock of the Rhymney Railway, and so, on 3rd November 1893, Cornelius Lundie was authorised to prepare plans and specifications and to invite tenders for the supply of four six-wheeled third class carriages and one brake van for use on the branch. The tenders received were considered by the Rhymney Board on 1st December, with that of the Metropolitan Carriage & Wagon Co. being accepted at £381 10s for the third class carriages and £369 10s for the brake. The four thirds completed in 1894 (Nos.6, 7, 28 and 80) were each 31ft 4in long. The passenger brake van formed part of a larger order for four such vehicles (Nos.81-84). Also supplied during 1894 was brake/third coach No.79.

Motive power for the service, on the other hand, could be supplied from existing resources in the form of locomotive No.1, an 0-6-0 tender engine built by Vulcan Foundry in 1857. It was one of six engines designated class 'A' in 1906 and was withdrawn in the first half of 1907, the entire class going between then and April 1908. No.6 of this class was also shedded at Senghenydd for a time.

The inaugural timetable was somewhat limited, consisting of only three Up and two Down trains, Mondays to Fridays, together with a third Down working on Saturdays. No Sunday service was provided, a feature that was to continue throughout the life of the branch.

This unbalanced service was soon altered to give three trains each way, Mondays to Saturdays, the working timetable for June 1895 being:

Plate 35 - Rhymney Railway Class 'A' 0-6-0 No.6. This engine was shedded at Senghenydd at one time.

	a.m	p.m	p.m
Caerphilly *dep*	9.00	4.42	6.30
Penyrheol	9.05	4.47	6.35
Aber	9.10	4.52	6.40
Senghenith *arr*	9.15	4.57	6.45

		SO	SX	
	a.m	p.m	p.m	p.m
Senghenith *dep*	8.10	2.15	3.10	5.13
Aber	8.15	2.20	3.15	5.17
Penyrheol	8.20	2.25	3.20	5.21
Caerphilly *arr*	8.25	2.30	3.25	5.25

By June 1901 the service had been expanded to six trains each way. A late evening round trip was added in 1903, with an unbalanced eighth working from Caerphilly joining it in the Summer of 1906.

In 1902 a set of four-wheeled coaches was formed into a train for service on the Senghenydd branch. The modern era, at least as far as lighting was concerned, was ushered in on 3rd October, when the Rhymney Board authorised the fitting of electric light equipment to these vehicles.

July 1906 saw a start being made on rebuilding of the twelve engines of the '45-56' class of 0-6-0STs, all of which had been built by Sharp, Stewart & Co. in 1884. The first of what then became class 'J' to be dealt with was No.53, which was then shedded at Senghenydd for passenger work, for which it was always kept in immaculate condition. Rebuilding was carried out at Caerphilly and involved the fitting of a replacement boiler and a redesigned cab.

At the time of the opening of the Aber branch the goods and mineral traffic of the Rhymney Railway was still largely in the hands of outside-framed 0-6-0 saddle tanks. The typical South Wales type - the 0-6-2T - was also represented, albeit in a similar format to the 0-6-0STs, in the shape of 47 engines of the '57' (later 'K') class introduced in 1890. Engines of this class were to make up the bulk of the allocation at Senghenydd.

The first modern 0-6-2 side tank locomotives did not appear on the Rhymney Railway until 1904 in the form of the six members of

Plate 36 - Senghenydd station with steam railcar and trailer and station staff posing for the camera, c.1910; a poor picture but included for its historical interest.

the '106-110' (later 'M') class, built by R Stephenson & Co. From then on, through to the Grouping in 1922, orders for new engines were dominated by this type.

Full details of all Rhymney Railway motive power can be found in Part 10 of *The Locomotives of the Great Western Railway*, published by the Railway Correspondence & Travel Society.

Steam railcars

The early years of this century saw a wave of enthusiasm in railway circles for self-propelled steam railcars. They were especially popular with the railways of South Wales, with the TVR leading the way, but with a number of other companies, including the ByR and the AD&R, also being represented. The Rhymney Railway, however, showed no great inclination to adopt 'motor cars' (as they were usually known in South Wales), Cornelius Lundie being notoriously conservative as far as locomotive design and development were concerned.

Things changed with the appointment of Ernest Prosser as General Manager of the Rhymney Railway in February 1905. On 3rd November of that year the Rhymney Board considered a report prepared by Prosser on the subject of motor cars and instructed him to make further enquires and to report back. The General Manager was greatly helped in this task by Carlton Hurry Riches who took up his appointment as the Rhymney Co.'s Locomotive Superintendent on 1st January 1906. Hurry Riches' father, Tom, was Locomotive Engineer of the TVR and a very powerful advocate of the merits of steam motor cars. An outline drawing of the proposed car (which was estimated to cost about £2,500) was submitted to the Rhymney Board at its meeting on 2nd November, when instructions were given for tenders to be invited for the construction of two of these vehicles.

The engine units for the cars were supplied by Hudswell Clarke & Co. of Leeds, the coach sections coming from Cravens Ltd. of Sheffield. The cars, numbered 1 and 2 in a separate series, were powerful enough to haul up to three 6-wheeled coaches. The engine unit was an 0-4-0 with outside cylinders and Walschaert's valve gear. The coach unit was supported at one end by a rear extension from the loco unit, and by an 8ft wheelbase bogie at the other, and could accommodate 64 passengers, all third class. Both vehicles were delivered in September 1907, one being shedded at Rhymney for use between there and Ystrad Mynach, the other going to Senghenydd for use on the Aber branch.

The arrival of the car at Senghenydd enabled a revised timetable to be introduced on the branch on 1st October 1907. This comprised nine trips each way, worked by a single car, starting from Senghenydd at 5.45am and finishing with the 10/05pm ex Caerphilly.

At the Rhymney Co.'s half-yearly meeting on 7th February 1908 the Chairman, Mr G L Clarke, noted that the cars had run about 6,000 miles, providing a more

The Aber Branch

Plate 37 - Steam railcar No.1 as built.

frequent service and improving the 'comfort and convenience of the public'. However, from the outset the 0-4-0 wheel arrangement of the engine unit had given cause for concern, it being found that the carriage section was not sufficiently supported by the locomotive frame. As a result both cars were taken out of service and the engine units altered to 0-4-2s, although the trailing wheels themselves were actually beneath the carriage section.

Alterations were made to the Aber branch service in 1st April 1908, when Beddau Halt opened for traffic. At the same time a new service was introduced over the Caerphilly to Machen line of the B&MR, worked by a Rhymney motor car in conjunction with the Caerphilly to Sengheyndd service. The Aber branch timetable continued to show nine workings each way until 1911 when an early evening round trip was added. This addition proved short lived, however, and did not appear in the timetable for the following year, but by 1915 the service was back to ten trips each way.

From 1908 a 6-wheel third class carriage No.26 (built at Cardiff in 1890) was allocated for use as a non-driving trailer with the motor cars. In the absence of a driving end, however, it was necessary for the car to run round its trailer at each end of its journey.

In 1910 motor car No.2 was withdrawn from service and the locomotive unit separated from the carriage section. The former was altered to an 0-6-0 configuration, complete with large rear bunker combined with water tank, and given the number 120. In this form it was used on the Aber branch passenger service for about a year before settling down as the regular Caerphilly goods yard pilot. The coach section was fitted with an additional bogie and numbered 114 in the company's ordinary carriage stock.

The annual mileages recorded for the motor cars between their introduction in 1907 and 1912 are shown in Table 1. It will be noted that the use of the surviving car (No.1) declined dramatically in 1911, but then staged a recovery in 1912.

Table 1 - Motor car annual mileage

1907	6,370	miles
1908	48,669	miles
1909	42,125	miles
1910	35,465	miles
1911	5,914	miles
1912	14,469	miles

At the opening of the new locomotive and carriage works at Caerphilly in December 1901 the Rhymney Co. had laid on a special works train for the benefit of employees who wished to continue to reside in Cardiff. On 4th October 1907 the company gave notice that this service would be withdrawn at the end of March 1908. However, by way of compensation the works train was re-routed to start from Abertridwr on the Aber branch, where it joined an existing Caerphilly to Senghenydd workmen's service. Old four-wheeled coaches, numbered in duplicate stock, were kept for this purpose. They were painted battleship grey and were without any form of heating.

In June 1912 the Rhymney Co. purchased nineteen six-wheeled coaches from the LSWR for use on the colliers' and workmen's trains. A further twelve coaches, for workmen only, were acquired from the Metropolitan District Railway in September 1914. Vehicles from these sources replaced the ancient four-wheelers on the Caerphilly works and Aber branch colliers' trains.

The Rhymney Railway, having been a late developer as far as steam railcars were concerned, was also somewhat late on the scene with what was generally the next stage of development - the auto-train. In 1915 a brake/third coach (No.20) was constructed at Caerphilly Works and fitted with driving gear (through the underframe) and a driving end. At the same time coach No.22, built at Caerphilly the previous year, was also fitted for auto-working. For motive

(Above) Plate 38 - No.1 in service at Senghenydd after rebuilding as an 0-4-2. Note the trailing wheels under the carriage section.

(Right) Plate 39 - Rhymney Railway carriages Nos.1 and 2 c.1913, probably displaced from colliers' trains by the purchase of second-hand stock from the LSWR in 1912.

power 2-4-2ST No.66, which was undergoing heavy repair at the time, was selected and appropriately equipped. No.66 was one of five engines built by Vulcan Foundry in 1890, three of the class having been converted to 0-6-2STs in 1908 and 1911. It had been works pilot at Caerphilly since 1909 and was now replaced in that duty by trailing tank No.120. Newly repainted, No.66 came out of the locomotive shops in October 1915, but it was not until the following December that the two coach auto-set was ready for traffic. Steam heating was added in 1919, the same year that a second auto-set - made up of coaches Nos.21 and 25 - was formed.

The high level of coal output that continued through the war years, coupled with the loss of men to the armed forces, led to a shortage of labour in many mining areas. Workmen's trains had featured in the Aber Valley since at least 1905, but the need to attract men into the mines from outside the valley became that much greater. On 4th August 1916 Mr Prosser informed his Directors that he had agreed to sell six old carriages to the Windsor Steam Coal Co. and the Lewis Merthyr Colliery Co. for £450 for use on a proposed workmen's service between Taffs Well and Windsor and Universal Collieries. The Board was informed on 3rd November that the agreement for running this service had been completed, and on 5th January 1917 Prosser reported the sale of two more coaches for this purpose.

Unlike those of many other local services the Aber branch timetable did not suffer a great deal of erosion during the war years. The service had reached a peak of ten workings each way in 1915, but by the time of the Armistice in November 1918, it was down to eight from Caerphilly and nine from Senghenydd. It was to remain at this level for much of the 1920s.

Motor car No.1 had continued to find worthwhile employment, albeit latterly on the northern part of the Rhymney system rather than on the Aber branch. However, in May 1919 it was withdrawn from traffic and subjected to the same treatment as had been given to Car No.2 in 1910. The former locomotive unit became trailing tank engine No.121, while the carriage section, with second bogie added, became brake/third No.119. In this form they returned to traffic in June 1919, locomotive No.121

The Aber Branch

Plate 40 - Former RR Class 'K' 0-6-2ST No.9 as GWR No.86.

(Right) Plate 41 - RR Class '57' 0-6-2ST No.83.

(Left) Plate 42 - RR Class 'J' 0-6-0ST No.53 at Bargoed. This engine worked the Aber branch prior to the introduction of steam railcars in 1907.

Locomotive and Train Working

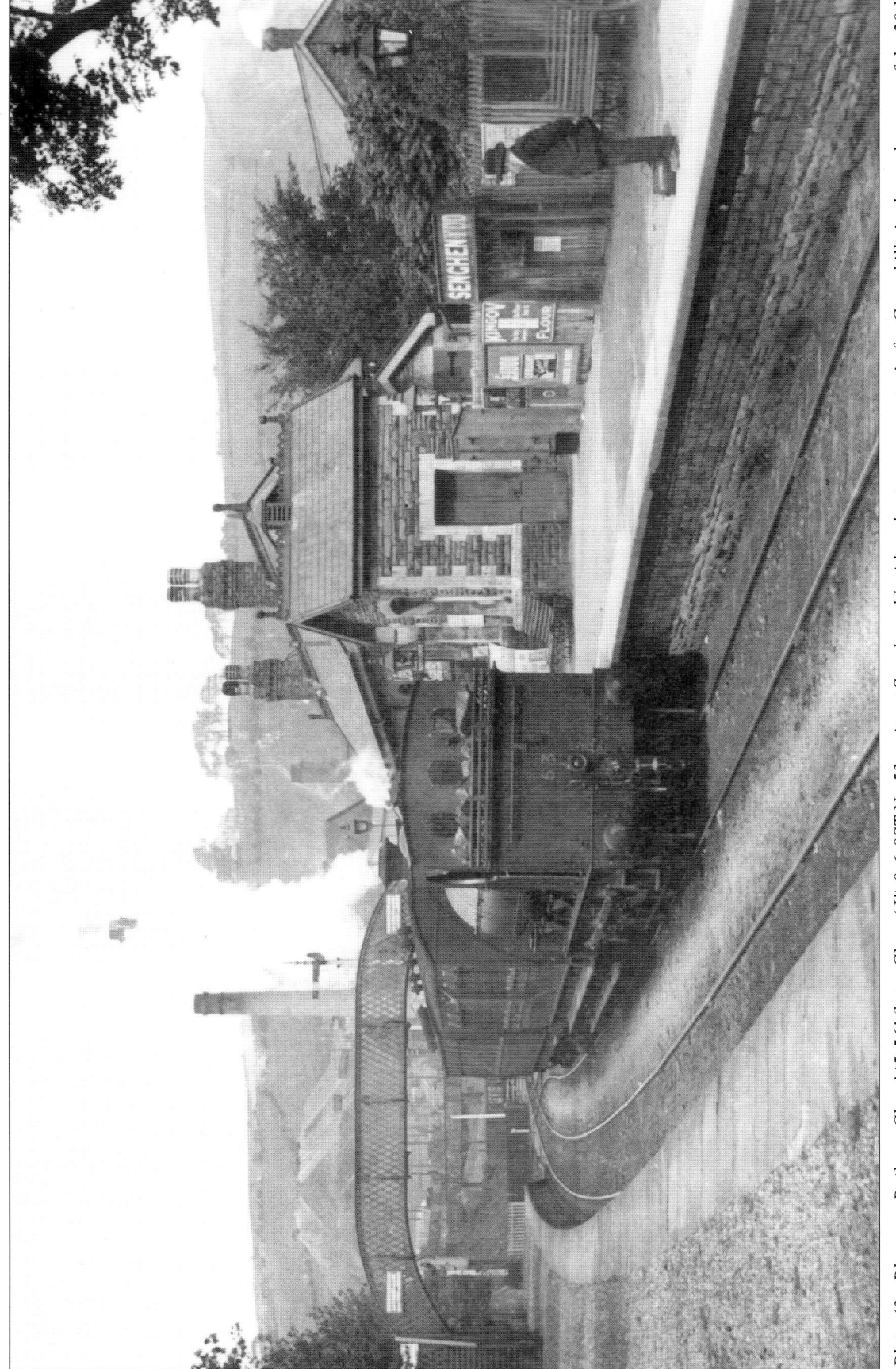

Plate 43 - Rhymney Railway Class '45-56' (later Class 'J') 0-6-0ST No.53 waits at Senghenydd with a short passenger train for Caerphilly in the early years of the 20th century. The station nameboard shows signs of having been altered from the earlier 'Senghenith' spelling.

53

becoming Works pilot, displacing sister engine No.120, which then returned to its former duties as Caerphilly yard pilot.

Post-grouping and the War years

At the Grouping in 1922 the most numerous locomotive class allocated to Senghenydd shed was the 0-6-2ST class 'K', of which there were no less than ten examples - Nos.57, 74, 80, 83, 93, 95, 99, 101, 103 and 104. Also present were four class 'A1' 0-6-2Ts (Nos. 10, 11, 26 and 117), built by R Stephenson & Co. and Hudswell, Clarke & Co. between 1910 and 1917. However, the Rhymney monopoly of motive power at the shed was soon undermined by an influx of former ByR engines. Of the total of 17 locomotives shedded at Senghenydd at 1st January 1926, no less than eleven were 0-6-2Ts of Barry origin, as listed in Table 2.

Auto-working using former Rhymney engines and auto-trailers continued on the Senghenydd branch (the name, it will be recalled, used by the GWR) after the Grouping, but had ceased by July 1925. Most trains were confined to the Senghenydd to Caerphilly run, but a number worked through to or from Cardiff. Trains were usually made up of two compartment coaches, which were stabled overnight at Senghenydd.

After remaining at eight Up and nine Down trains since 1918, an additional round trip was added to the Senghenydd branch passenger timetable in 1927. This proved to be the start of a gradual increase in the service, a further return working being added from 24th September 1928 and another from 20th July 1931. By July 1933 it had reached its highest level yet with 12 departures from Caerphilly and 13 from Senghenydd. The service remained at this level until the introduction of the emergency timetable in September 1939.

The GWR working timetable for September 1928 included a total of 12 'set numbers' for goods and mineral workings from Senghenydd Depot. The timetable gave only the first working of the day for each set number, subsequent movements being dictated by 'Control' to meet the vicissitudes of the coal trade. Of the workings listed Set No.S.10 was the branch goods from Senghenydd to Aber Junction at 10.00am. Only two set numbers involved mineral workings from the Senghenydd branch itself (S.21 at 4/35pm and S.23 at 11/25pm), whilst the others were either light engine workings to Aber Junction, where traffic was picked up for various collieries or other junctions, or started out on workmen's trains before taking up similar duties.

On the closure of Senghenydd locomotive depot in May 1931 its allocation was divided between Radyr and Cardiff Cathays sheds.

Table 2 - Senghenydd Locomotive Allocation, 1926

GWR No.	ByR No.	ByR Class	Built by	Date
198	6	B	Sharp, Stewart & Co.	1888
207	13	B	Sharp, Stewart & Co.	1889
209	15	B	Sharp, Stewart & Co.	1889
211	17	B	Sharp, Stewart & Co.	1889
212	18	B	Sharp, Stewart & Co.	1889
225	25	B	Sharp, Stewart & Co.	1890
230	30	B	Sharp, Stewart & Co.	1890
240	42	B1	Sharp, Stewart & Co.	1890
250	59	B1	Vulcan Foundry	1892
254	63	B1	Vulcan Foundry	1892
267	111	B1	Sharp, Stewart & Co.	1900

The six ex Rhymney engines were:

GWR No.	RR No.	RR Class	Built by	Date
31	2	R	R. Stephenson & Co.	1907
41	45	R	Beyer Peacock & Co.	1921
87	57	K	Vulcan Foundry	1890
114	80	K	Sharp, Stewart & Co.	1897
115	81	K	Sharp, Stewart & Co.	1897
147	104	K	Neilson, Reid	1900

Of the ex Rhymney Railway engines Nos.31 and 41 were 0-6-2Ts, while the remainder were 0-6-2STs.

Plate 44 - A private owner coal wagon built for the Universal Colliery Co. and photographed 'ex-works' by the Gloucester Railway Carriage & Wagon Co. in March 1897.

Cathays then supplied the engines for the branch passenger service. Gradually the pre-grouping types gave way to standard GWR classes on goods and minerals workings, with class '56XX' 0-6-2Ts predominating.

The emergency passenger service timetable, brought in on 25th September 1939, cut back the Caerphilly to Senghenydd passenger train service to nine Up and ten Down trains. This proved but a temporary setback, however, as an additional round trip was added from March 1940. From July 1941 twelve trains were run each way, with auto-trains reappearing on the branch from this date. Class '64XX' 0-6-0PTs were employed for this purpose, there being no fewer than six members of this class at Cathays in December 1947. The auto trains catered for third class travel only.

An interesting development during the war years was the introduction, from 7th April 1941, of the Senghenydd to Llanbradach Colliery workmen's service, reversing at Caerphilly in both directions. The Down train left Senghenydd at 5.47am, arriving at Llanbradach Colliery at 6.25am, while in the opposite direction the 6.50am ex Llanbradach ran through to branch terminus. On Saturdays the 3/17pm train from Llanbradach also ran through to Senghenydd, but during the week its passengers were obliged to change trains at Caerphilly. In the early 1950s this train was formed of three four-wheeled coaches: No.2774, a 25ft five-compartment third; No.285, a 26ft brake third (formerly all third); and No.721, a 27ft four compartment third (formerly first/second class composite). This train ceased to run in 1952. Workmen's coaches were also added to certain ordinary service trains. In 1952 No.4023, an ex TVR trailer originally constructed as steam railcar No.14 in 1906, replaced a clerestory roofed coach that had previously been employed on this duty.

Post-War and British Railways

The immediate post-war years saw the passenger timetable reach a new peak, with 15 trains each way, the service remaining at this level even through the restrictions brought on by the coal shortage following the severe winter of 1946/47. During the early 1950s the branch auto train was usually formed of ex Cardiff Railway vehicles, including Nos.142 and 143 (originally steam railcars) and 144.

In October 1952, after much careful research and planning, the Western Region of British Railways brought out a document with the rather misleading title of *Costs of Passenger Train Services*, dealing specifically with the local services radiating from Cardiff and Bridgend. The central focus of this report was the radical proposal for the introduction of a regular interval service on the main Barry to Treherbert/Merthyr route via Cardiff and Pontypridd. Unfortunately, it proved impractical to extend this principle to the Cardiff to Rhymney service because of the need to maintain connections with other services at Bargoed (Newport to Brecon) and Hengoed (Pontypool Road to Neath). Not surprisingly, the document also concluded that such a service would also be impractical on the Senghenydd

Plate 45 - The Senghenydd to Llanbradach colliers' train referred to in the text awaiting departure from Senghenydd on 21st May 1951. The train is hauled by ex TVR Class 'A' 0-6-2T No.360.

The Aber Branch

Plate 46 - Class '64XX' 0-6-0PT No.6423 at Senghenydd coupled next to ex Taff Vale Railway trailer No.4023 and ex Cardiff Railway auto-cars Nos.143 and 144.

Senghenydd, 12th May 1952

Plate 47 - Exchange of single line tokens is just about to take place at Senghenydd signal box as a Down train departs for Caerphilly. The goods yard is host to a solitary van.

Plate 48 - Class '56XX' 0-6-2T No.6603 prepares to leave with a Down workmen's train.

Senghenydd, 12th May 1952

branch, and that the established pattern of auto-trains should therefore continue. The new timetable was introduced on 21st September 1953, but it was not until 27th June 1966, two years after the withdrawal of the Senghenydd to Caerphilly trains, that a regular interval service was introduced between Cardiff, Caerphilly and Rhymney.

To work the auto-trains under the new timetable class '45XX' 2-6-2Ts were drafted in and appeared on Caerphilly to Senghenydd trains, alongside class '64XX' 0-6-0PTs. In addition, eighteen third class compartment coaches (seven of Diagram A41 and eleven of Diagram A42) were converted to auto working. One of these, coupled to an auto trailer (usually an A27 dating from 1928), was used on the Senghenydd branch service.

Dieselisation

A further report appeared on 31st March 1955, entitled *Proposed Dieselisation of Cardiff Branch Passenger Services*. This envisaged the replacement of steam by diesel multiple units on the Cardiff Valleys passenger services, including the Senghenydd branch. Trials of the Derby-built units (later class '116') commenced in the Rhymney Valley on 16th October 1957. The first Cardiff Valleys services went over the dmu operation on 13th January 1958, with the Rhymney section following suit on 21st April, under Stage 4 of the scheme. However, it was not until Monday, 9th June - the day that diesel fuelling facilities were brought into use at Cardiff Cathays depot -

that conversion of the Senghenydd branch to diesel operation was completed. It is thought that the last scheduled steam auto-train on the branch was the 10.45am from Senghenydd-Cardiff (Bute Road), hauled by 0-6-0PT No.6416, on the preceding Saturday.

The passenger service timetable remained much as before, however, with 15 trains each way working at irregular intervals, in connection with the main Cardiff to Rhymney service. This pattern remained in force until the summer timetable, introduced on 18th June 1962, when, in an attempt to reduce costs, a drastic reduction was made in a number of loss-making services in the Cardiff area. The number of trains between Caerphilly and Senghenydd was reduced from 15 each way to 11 Up (cut to 10 from 17th June 1963) and 10 Down trains. Most of this decline was accounted for by workings withdrawn in the evening period, with the last Up train of the revised timetable leaving Caerphilly at 6.53pm and returning from Senghenydd at 7.17pm. Apart from discouraging use of the service for leisure purposes, this cutback also hit commuters to Cardiff who might have had to work late and people making connections at Cardiff from further afield. This reduced timetable then continued to apply until the end of the passenger service in June 1964.

Radyr Shed was closed to steam from 26th July 1965, but continued to function as a stabling point for diesel locomotives supplied by Cardiff Canton depot after this date. The closure of Radyr marked the end of regular steam

Plate 49 - On 31st July 1965, Class '56XX' 0-6-2T No.6643 hauls the 'Rambling 56' enthusiasts' excursion past the remains of Penyrheol station on its way to Senghenydd.

working in the Cardiff Valleys.

The surviving section of the Senghenydd branch was host to a final steam-hauled passenger working on 31st July 1965. This enthusiasts' excursion - christened the 'Rambling 56' - was organised by the Monmouthshire Railway Society and comprised a 4-coach train powered by class '56XX' 0-6-2T No.6643. In addition to Windsor Colliery, its itinerary took in the Walnut Tree Junction to Aber Junction line, Walnut Tree Viaduct and Dowlais Cae Harris, en route from Cardiff General to Newport High St.

Regular diesel operation of mineral traffic on the Senghenydd branch had commenced in 1964, with the arrival of English Electric Type '3' (later class '37') 1750 HP Co-Cos at Radyr. Two of these locomotives had been loaned from Sheffield for trials in 1962, their first appearance in the Rhymney Valley being on 4th October of that year. Local trip working instructions for 18th April 1966 gave two Radyr to Windsor Colliery workings (Saturdays excepted): H06 departing Radyr at 5.20am and returning from Windsor Colliery at 7.35am, and H13 from Radyr at 9.50am, returning at 12/10pm.

In their last years coal trains from Windsor Colliery were worked to Nantgarw Coke Ovens, entailing a reversal at Radyr Junction. Three trains were usually timetabled, the Up trains running from Radyr Junction and Down working through to Nantgarw. The final working timetable, commencing on 4th October 1976, gave the following times on the branch:

	a.m	a.m	p.m
Aber Junction *dep*	8.21	11.48	2.10
Windsor Colliery *arr*	8.33	12.00nn	2.22
	a.m	p.m	p.m
Windsor Colliery *dep*	9.44	1.11	4.06
Aber Junction *arr*	10.01	1.28	4.23

An RC&TS excursion worked by a six-car dmu ran over the branch to Windsor Colliery on 18th March 1972 as part of a somewhat eventful tour of former Rhymney Railway lines. Approaching the site of Abertridwr station the train was forced to come to an abrupt halt by a number of objects placed on the line, including a large oil drum, a tyre and, somewhat disturbingly, a pushchair containing a small child! The way having been cleared the dmu proceeded, albeit cautiously, to the end of the line, just beyond Windsor Colliery, where it reversed for an unimpeded run back to Aber Junction.

The last coal trains from Windsor Colliery on 4th December 1976 were worked by the customary class '37' Co-Co locomotives. However, there was one more revenue working over the branch on 15th April 1977 when a class '47' Co-Co hauled National Coal Board diesel engine No.27655 from Windsor Colliery to Radyr, en route to

Plate 50 - Class '47' No.47 237 on a Cwm Bargoed to Aberthaw 'merry-go-round' coal train passes Aber Junction on 3rd April 1978. The junction layout and signalling is intact despite the branch to Windsor Colliery having been closed the previous year.

Mountain Ash.

As we have seen, Aber Junction Halt continued in use after the withdrawal of the Senghenydd branch passenger service in 1964. From 13th May 1985 the service at Aber increased to half-hourly, Mondays to Saturdays, with the introduction of additional trains between Cardiff and Ystrad Mynach. Some trains also turned back for Cardiff at Aber, making use of the crossover near the site of the former junction.

However, this practice ended with the closure of Aber Junction signal box in May 1987 and the installation of a new crossover to the east of Caerphilly station. This enabled terminating trains to be turned back at Caerphilly, allowing the introduction of an extra two trains, each hour, between there and Cardiff, giving a 15 minutes frequency over this section of the Rhymney line for much of the day. This level of service evidently proved over-optimistic as from 30th May 1994 the Rhymney Valley service was reduced to three trains per hour, one to Rhymney, one to Bargoed and one as far as Caerphilly. Unfortunately this resulted in an uneven pattern (ie. 20 and 40 minutes intervals) at Aber and stations to Bargoed.

Accident

Details of one accident, a runaway, are to hand. It occurred during the morning of 25th February 1938 at the Windsor Colliery sidings, Abertridwr.

The GWR form for a 'Report of Collision, Derailment, Fire, Flood, etc.' carries the details although the final signature, for A W Hollingworth, was 5th September 1938.

1. Date: 25th February 1938.
2. Time: 8.45a.m.
3. Location Abertridwr, Windsor Colliery, 11m.0½c.

4. Description of Occurrence:
Y.29 assisted by a banker engine, pulled up above Colliery gate in readiness to put off 21 loaded wagons into the Colliery Sidings. Brakes were put down and the train proceeded into the siding. Whilst this was being done a portion of the train became uncoupled and these wagons ran wild and collided with 18 wagons which were standing below the screen. All the wagons then ran the length of the Colliery Siding through the gate and into the stopblock at 11m. 45c. About 25 wagons became derailed. The block was knocked out of position.

5. Particulars of damage
Weighbridge, stopblock and gate damaged.

Figure 23 - GWR luggage label.

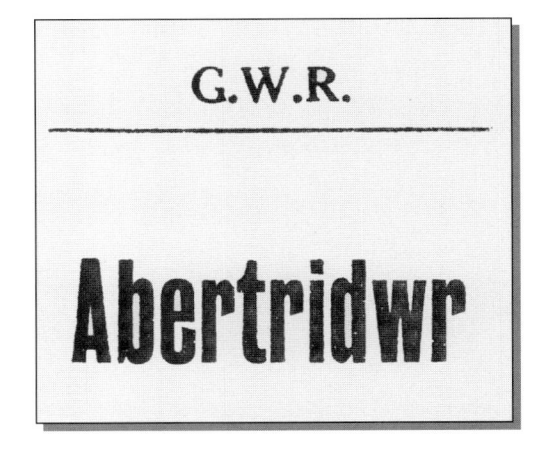

The Aber Branch

Plate 51 - The Senghenydd branch auto-train, hauled by 0-6-0PT No.6435, passes Caerphilly East.

Plate 52 - A view of Senghenydd station from the Caerphilly end with an auto-train in the Down platform.

60

Locomotive and Train Working

Plate 53 - Aber Junction looking south, as seen from a Senghenydd to Caerphilly dmu which is just about to cross onto the main line. Class '56XX' 0-6-2T No.6635 shunts the Up side of the yard on 28th September 1963.
Plate 54 - The sidings to the south-west of Aber Junction on 3rd April 1978. Class '37' No.37 227 and brake van are en route to Radyr, whilst No.37 282 heads a Radyr to Bargoed working.

61

6
Along the Line

In common with other independent railway companies in South Wales, the Rhymney Railway relied upon the local convention of 'Up' being 'up the valley' and 'Down' being 'down to the sea', rather than relating such matters to a somewhat remote metropolis. Our journey over the Aber branch from Caerphilly is therefore in the Up direction. Distances are given in miles and chains and are measured from the terminus in Cardiff in accordance with GWR practice. The date of our journey is indeterminate so as to be able to record all of the features that existed on the branch over the years.

As we have seen, at the opening of the Aber branch through to Senghenydd in 1890, Caerphilly station (8m 20ch) was a simple wayside affair with Up and Down platforms and a small goods yard alongside. The station building, on the Down side, was a two-storey stone-built structure, with a hipped roof and a rather ungainly canopy for the protection of intending passengers from the elements. A typical Rhymney waiting shelter with a mono-pitched roof and no canopy adorned the Up platform. By 1903 an extra platform had been added on the Up side, to the west of the bridge carrying the Cardiff road over the railway, this being used, according to G A Sekon (alias G A Nokes of the *Railway Magazine*), to accommodate GWR trains running between Pontypridd and Newport. This platform was served by a separate footpath down from the road over the railway, the clearances under the bridge being too restricted for a link from the original platform. Following an inspection of the line by the Directors on 24th July 1903, it was recommended that a replacement shelter be provided on the Up side, and that the road bridge be altered so as to enable the two Up platforms to be joined together. In the event, nothing was done as these proposals were soon overtaken by the much grander rebuilding scheme, which has already been described in Chapter Three.

Caerphilly became a 'closed' station (ie. access and egress controlled by ticket collectors) on 22nd March 1926.

A new Caerphilly East signal box was added in 1902, being reported as ready for inspection on 3rd November. This box, containing 39 working and 3 spare levers, was swept aside in the station rebuilding. The new box, opened in 1913 with 111 working and 21 spare levers, lasted until 20th July 1964.

Plate 55 - Caerphilly station looking towards Senghenydd on 13th September 1956. Aber branch trains generally arrived at Platform No.2, the trailing crossover enabling such trains to set back into Platform No.1.

Along the Line

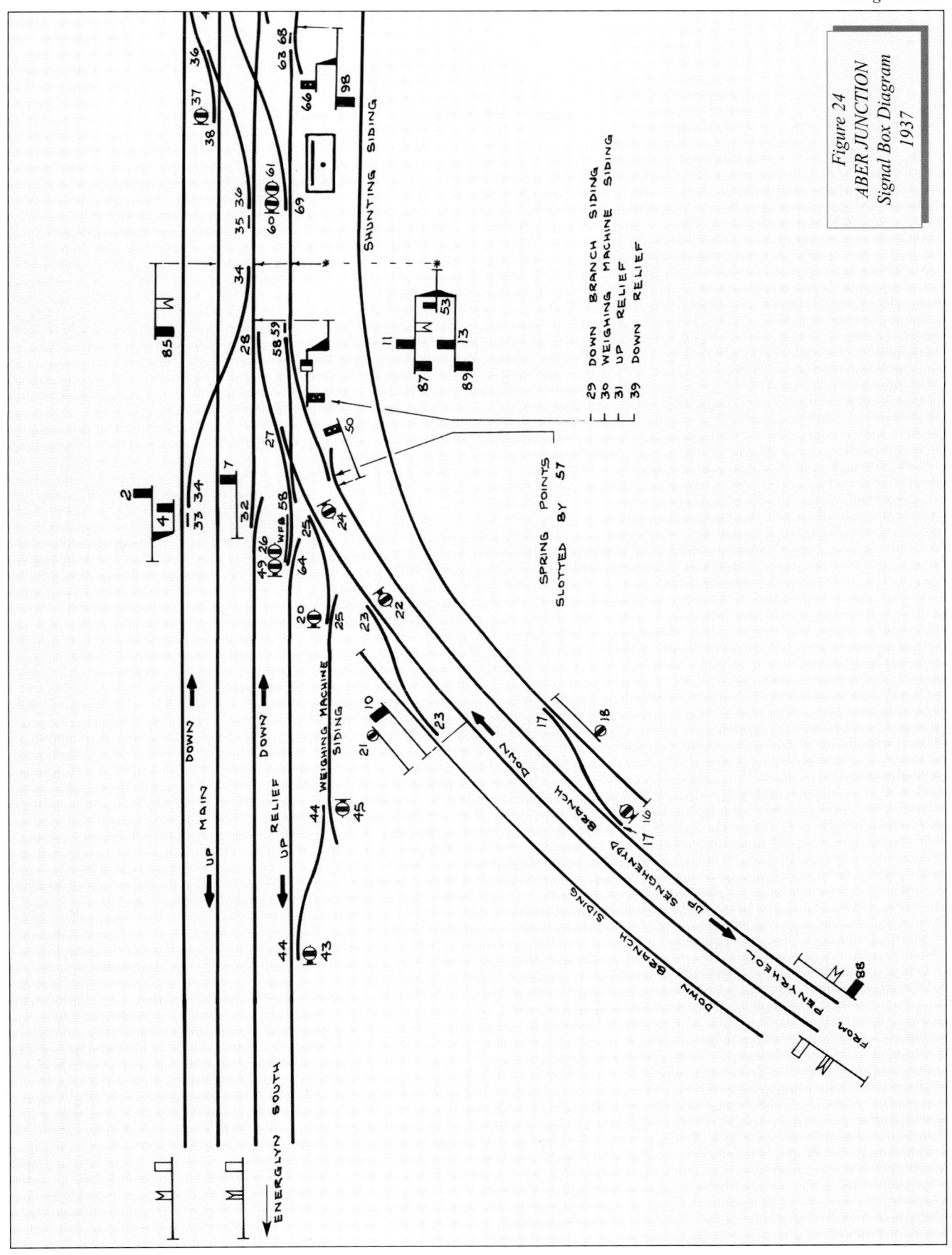

Figure 24
ABER JUNCTION
Signal Box Diagram
1937

The Aber Branch

Plate 56 - Aber Junction on 11th June 1962, showing the the signal box authorised by the GWR in 1947. This view is looking along the Rhymney main line towards the junction with the Senghenydd branch.

Leaving the confines of Caerphilly station, the Aber branch train was soon rattling over the points at Caerphilly West Junction (8m 36ch). In 1890 this was a simple double junction, the signal box dating from 1886.

As part of the Caerphilly station rebuilding scheme two sets of double lines were provided between Caerphilly East and West Junctions, with the two coming together at the latter place in a somewhat complex arrangement under the control of a new signal box, containing 52 working and 4 spare levers. Caerphilly West signal box was closed on 29th September 1968.

From Caerphilly West Junction the Rhymney main line curved to the north towards Beddau (later Aber Junction) Halt. A substantial corrugated iron 'Pagoda' style shelter was provided on the Up platform by the GWR. Originally built with timber platforms, 130ft long, the halt was reconstructed and lengthened to 300ft in 1954 (*see Chapter Four*). The new corrugated iron waiting shelters, of somewhat utilitarian design, coupled with the prefabricated concrete platforms, gave the rebuilt halt a rather austere and uninviting appearance.

Strictly speaking, Aber Junction consisted of two junctions: Walnut Tree Branch Junction and Aber Junction itself. In their original form the two were double junctions, with short lengths of double line beyond each junction on the Walnut Tree and Aber branches. Only two sidings existed in 1875, one trailing off the Down line between the two junctions, and the other, with trailing connections to both Up and Down lines, on the Caerphilly line.

A new signal box was provided in 1893, and by the turn of the century an additional Down passenger line had been added, together with various sidings on all of the lines radiating from Aber Junction. However, as has been seen (*in Chapter Three*), the major changes were made between 1904 and the outbreak of World War I. At its peak in 1915 a substantial array of sidings, known as Beddau Sidings, existed on the Walnut Tree branch, just south of the junction, together with a number of dead-end sidings each side of the Rhymney line. Quadruple track had been provided on the Rhymney main line between Aber Junction and Llanbradach, with an Up mineral relief line running from Beddau Sidings to join the Aber branch.

In its original form the Aber branch had terminated in two sets of loop sidings, one serving Penyrheol (or Hendredenny Colliery), and the other Tir Gibbon Colliery. George Williams is reported to have struck coal at the former on 23rd August 1860, but by 1863 the mine had passed to Messrs. David and Sloper and had been abandoned by 1887. Tir Gibbon was being worked by Williams, Lewis & Co. in 1865, before passing to the Energlyn Coal Co. It was abandoned in December 1876.

To page 70✯

Figure 25
PENYRHEOL GWR Property Plan

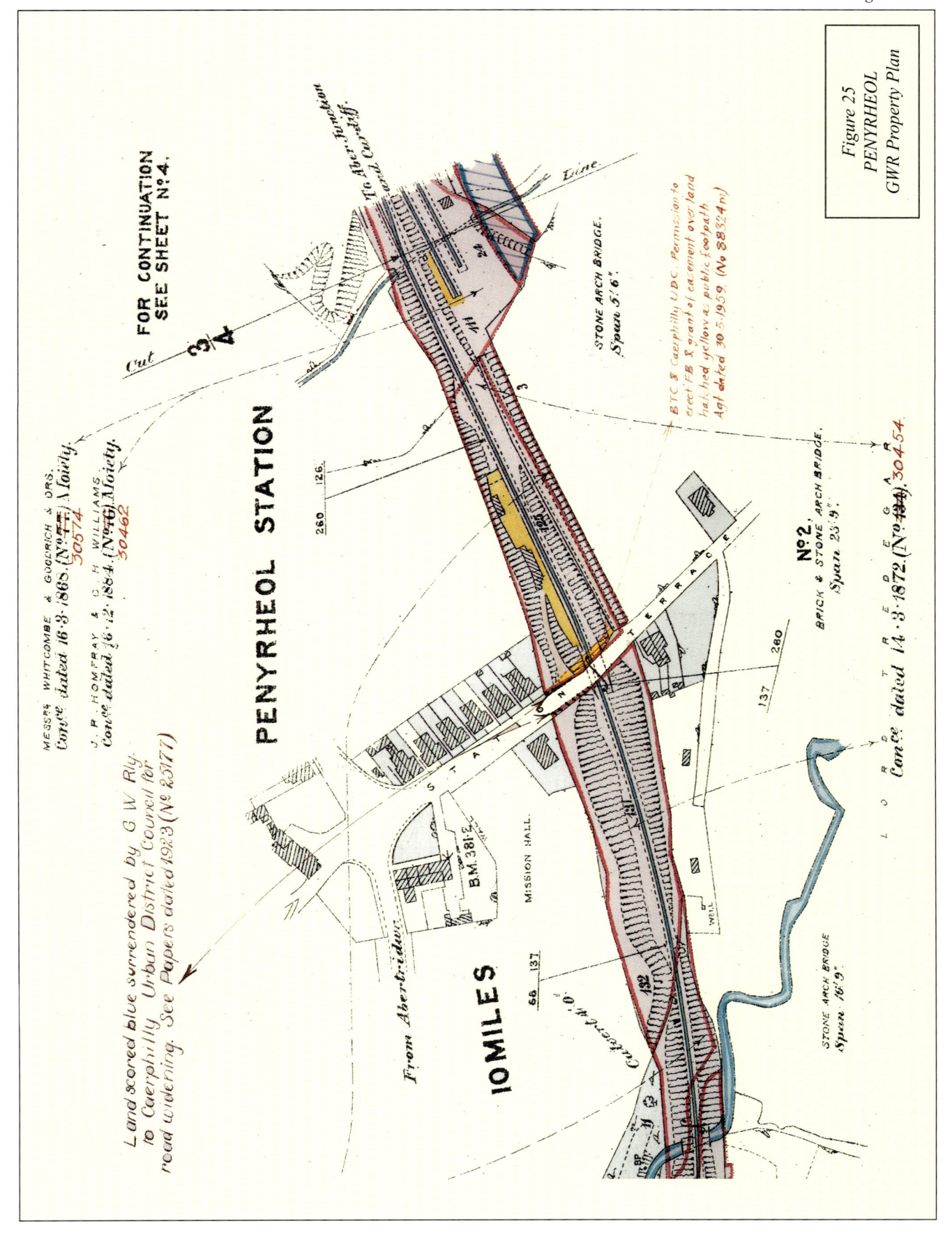

The Aber Branch

Plate 57 - The signalman waits with the single-line token at Penyrheol signal box on 28th September 1963.

Plate 58 - Penyrheol station, towards Aber Junction and Caerphilly, looking somewhat forlorn and neglected towards the end of the passenger service in 1963.

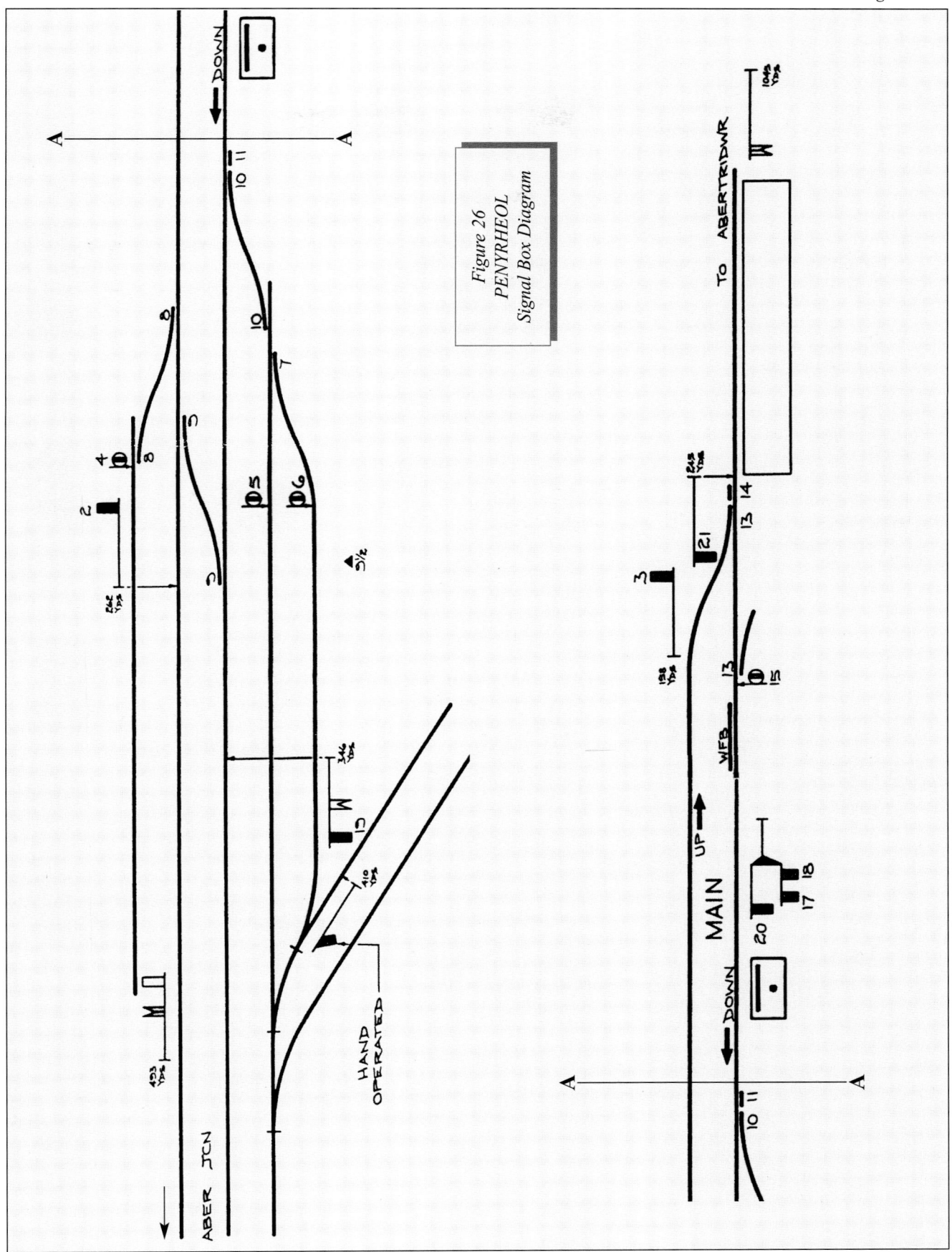

Figure 26
PENYRHEOL Signal Box Diagram

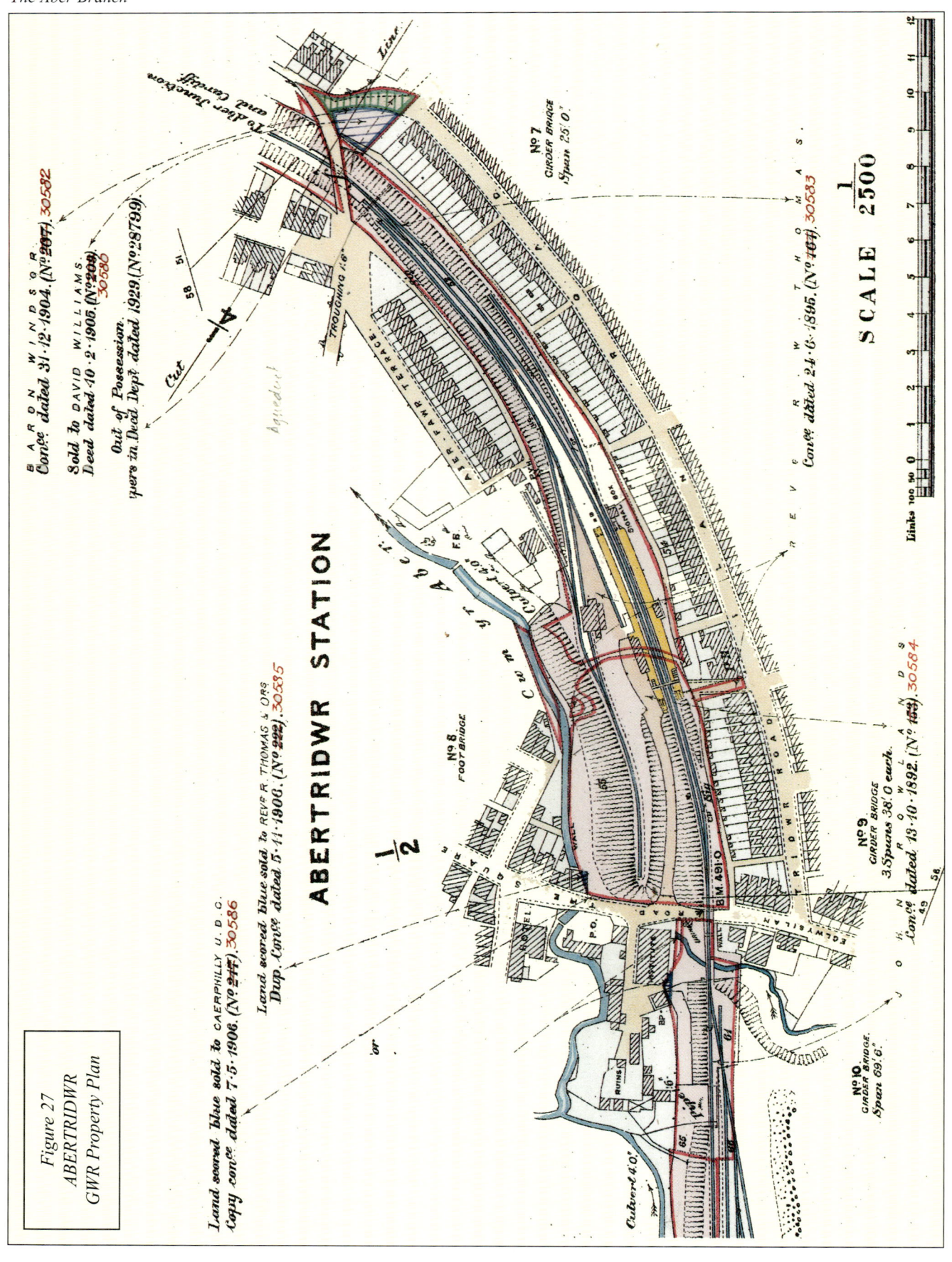

The Aber Branch

*Figure 27
ABERTRIDWR
GWR Property Plan*

Along the Line

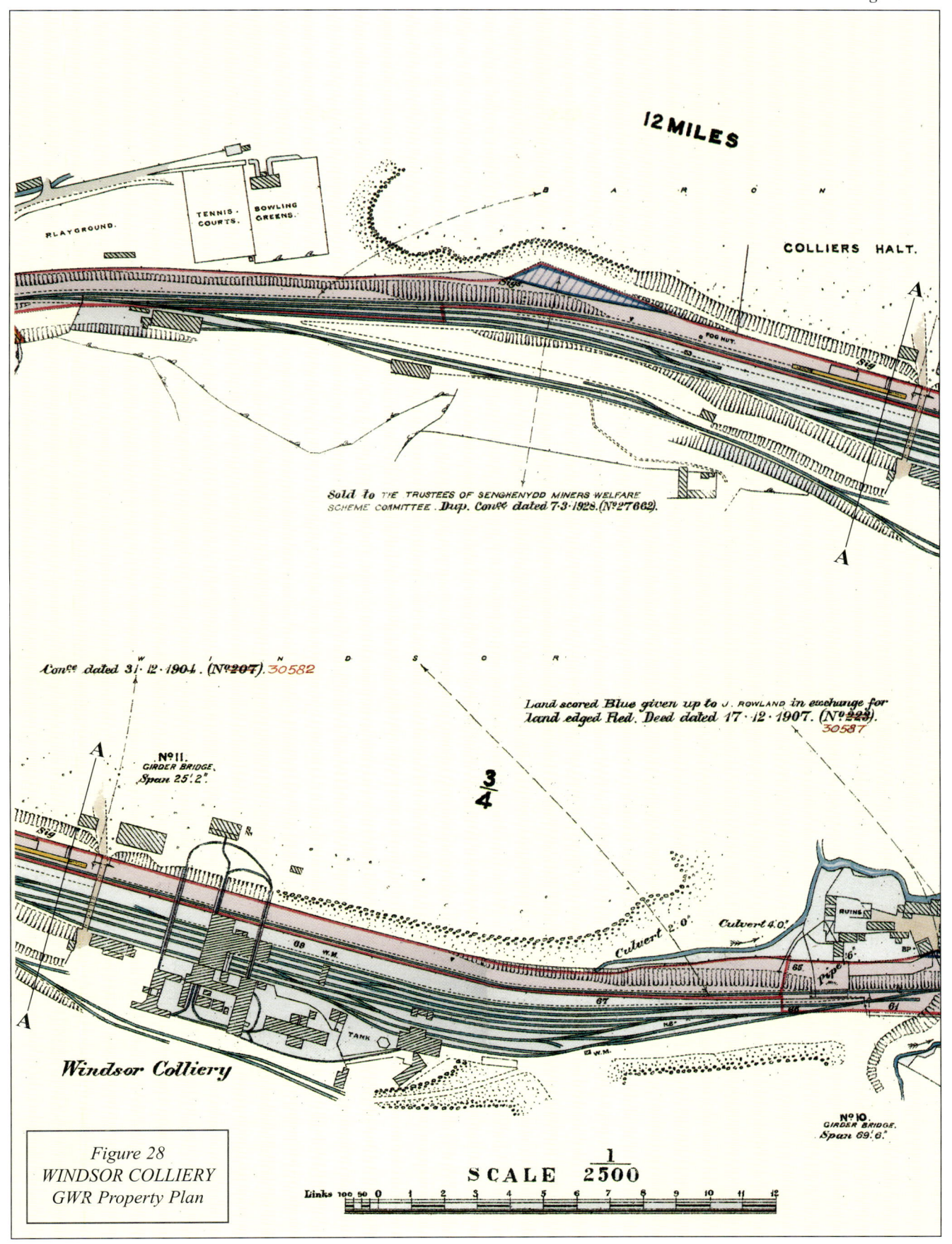

**Figure 28
WINDSOR COLLIERY
GWR Property Plan**

The Aber Branch

In later years extensive storage sidings - known as Aber Junction Sidings - were provided on the north side of the Aber branch, midway between Aber Junction and Penyrheol station, the whole being crossed by the ByR's Penyrheol Viaduct. The double track section between Aber Junction and Penyrheol signal box was singled on 14th June 1964, when the latter box was also closed. Most of the surviving sidings were taken out of use during 1964.

Penyrheol station (9m 68ch) was situated on the single line just beyond the end of the double track section from Aber Junction. Built in coursed stone with a gabled slated roof, the neat single storey station building was typical of the branch stations. Immediately beyond the end of the platform the line passed under a stone arched bridge, built wide enough for double track.

From Penyrheol the line ran through a wooded and sparsely populated part of the Aber Valley, in a generally north-westerly direction, keeping close company with the river and the main road. It then bore to the west, passing through a cutting and turning to the west, then turned towards the north before arriving at Abertridwr station (11m 35ch).

Abertridwr was the only intermediate passing place on the branch. Platforms were provided on each side of the passing loop, with the stone-built station building at the mid point on the Down side. A matching shelter graced the Up platform, with a lattice footbridge providing access

---

Transcript of letter from Swindon Private Siding Agreement file 18701. The Agreement was terminated from 1st July 1977.

'Great Western Railway
Divisional Engineer's Office
Queen Street, Cardiff

March 4th 1924

Dear Sir,

Windsor Steam Coal Company - Sidings at Abertridwr

I am obliged for your letter of the 3rd instant and will arrange to remove the junction to the above sidings on Sunday next, the 9th instant.

I assume that in this case as the existing connection will simply be reproduced in a new position and be moved 250 feet only, it will not be necessary to submit the usual plan to the Ministry of Transport.

Yours faithfully, etc

J C Lloyd, Esq.
Paddington.'

Plate 59 - The approach to Abertridwr as seen from a north-bound train on 17th August 1963.

Plate 60 - The waiting shelter on the Up platform at Abertridwr on a very wet day in 1963.

Figure 29 ABERTRIDWR Signal Box Diagram

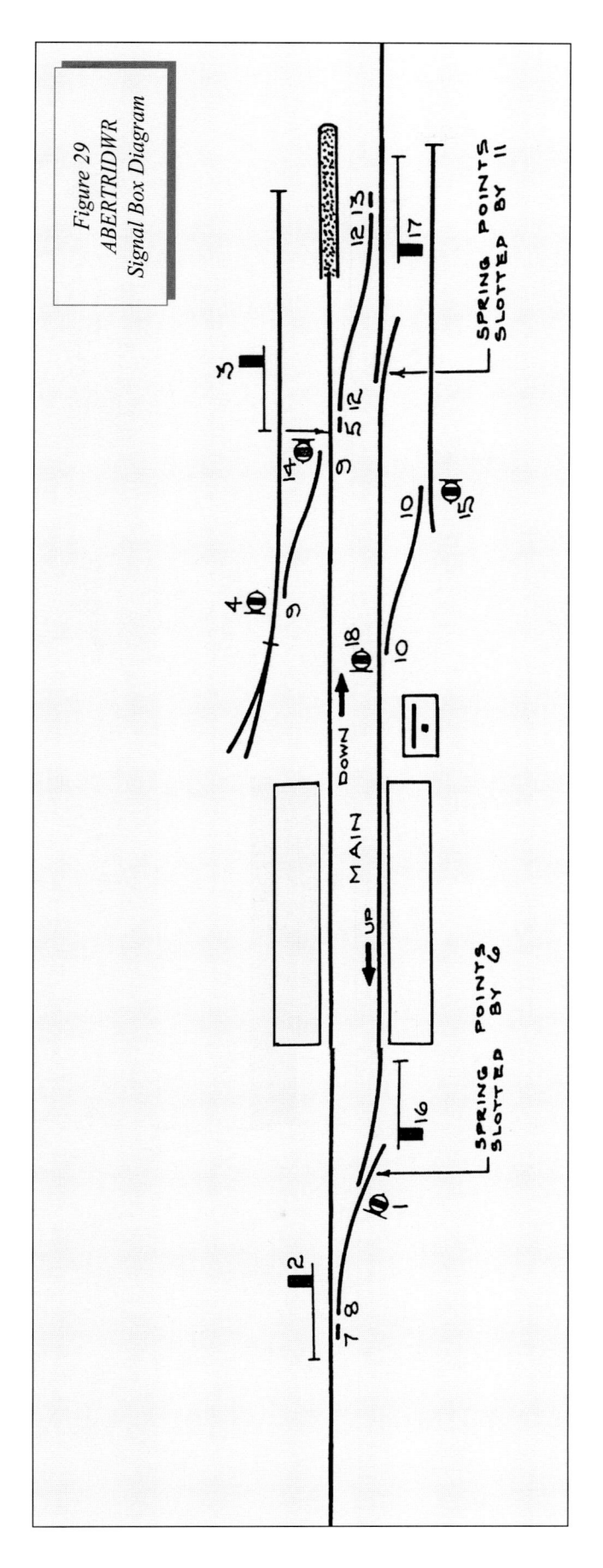

across the lines for passengers. The signal box (11m 32ch) was situated on the Up side, just south of the platform.

The goods yard was on the Down side of the line, to the rear of the passenger accommodation, access being by means of a trailing connection off the Down line. The yard consisted of a short dead-end siding, together with a longer siding from which a loop served a stone-built goods shed. A private siding, provided under an agreement dated 23rd July 1904, ran back from the outer side of the loop to reach a yard belonging to T Williams & Co. This siding agreement was terminated in 1934.

Another siding trailed off the Up line. In 1898 a tramway had connected this siding to Cwm-byr Quarry on the mountainside to the south of the station. This link had gone by 1915, although at this date a tramway still ran from the quarry to the nearest public road.

In addition to the sand drag, already referred to (*see Chapter Four*), the gradient of 1 in 58 through the station necessitated the provision of catch points at the Caerphilly end of the Up loop.

The Appendix to the Working Timetable for November 1926 included the following special instructions:

'*Crossing trains - Electric Train Staff Working, Abertridwr*

When it is necessary to cross an Up Freight Train which is assisted by a Bank Engine with a Down train at Abertridwr, the Fireman of the Bank Engine of the Up Train must, if the Train has been brought to a stand and the Driver of the Bank Engine has satisfied himself that the whole of the Train is in clear of the catch points on the Up Loop, at once proceed with the Staff to the Signal Box.

Working Up Line Traffic to Abertridwr

The connection to the Goods Yard at Abertridwr is from the Down Line only. Up traffic for Abertridwr conveyed on Trains worked by one Engine must be taken through to Senghenydd, from which place it must be brought back and put off on the Down journey. An Up Train assisted by a Bank Engine in the rear can detach traffic at Abertridwr, and as far as practicable traffic for that place should be conveyed on such Trains, formed at the rear so that the Bank Engine can propel the traffic into the Sidings.'

Little changed at Abertridwr until the 'rationalisation' era that followed the publication of the Beeching Report in 1963, with its emphasis on the concerted recovery of redundant assets. The outer line of the loop siding and part of the long dead-end siding were taken out of use on 8th March 1964. The points at the Caerphilly end of the passing loop and the goods yard head shunt followed on 14th June, these changes coinciding with the closure of the signal box.

The Aber Branch

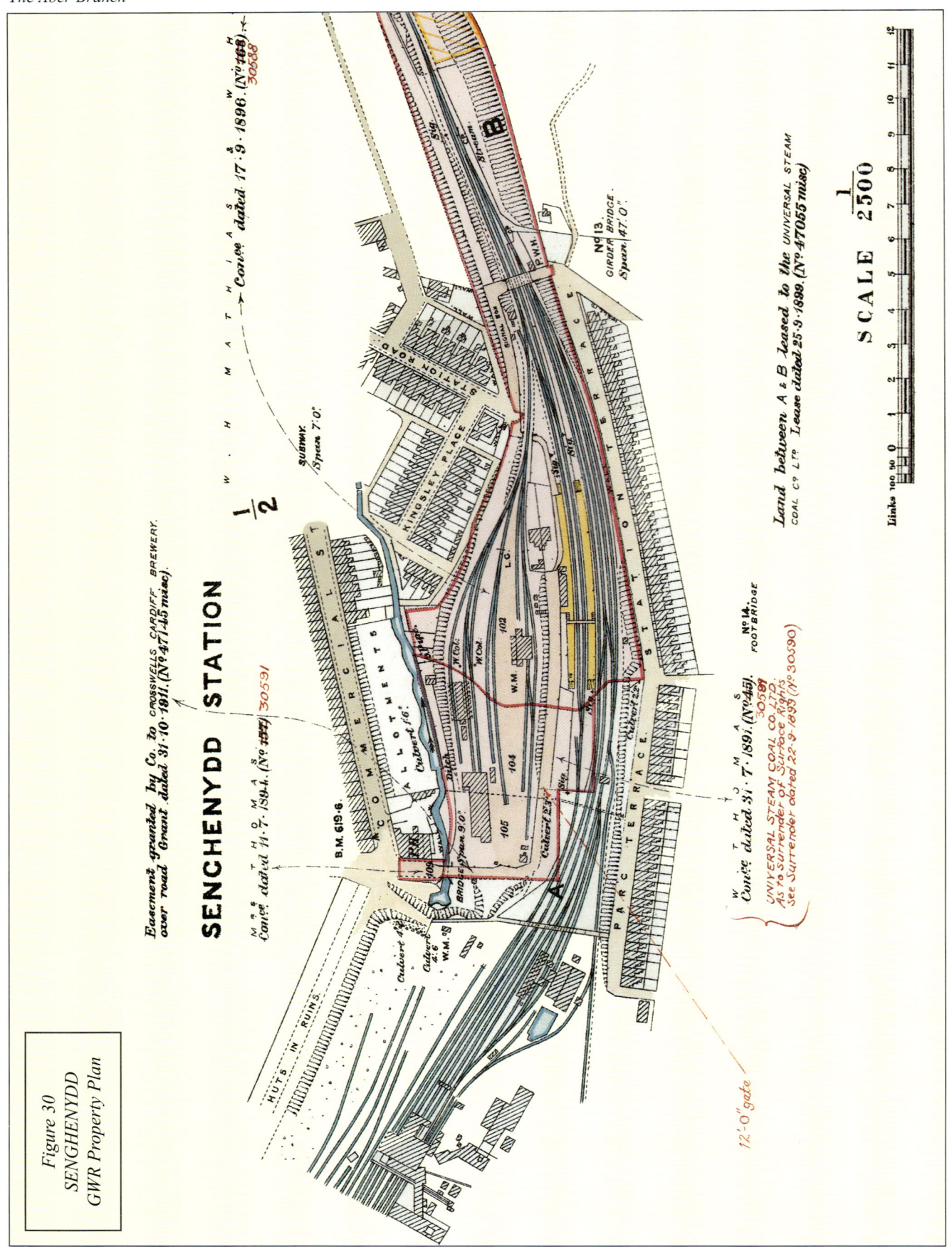

Figure 30
SENGHENYDD
GWR Property Plan

72

As a result, access to the goods yard was obtained by means of the former Down line, the entrance points being controlled by a ground frame. All lines, except the former Up loop line, were removed in March 1965.

Immediately beyond the upper points of Abertridwr passing loop the line ran onto a three-span girder bridge or 'viaduct' over a stream and side road. After crossing another bridge, it passed into a cutting, originally through a wooded area, curving to run almost due north at the same time.

After 1903 the western side of the line at this point was given over to the south junction to Windsor Colliery sidings. The colliery sidings themselves ran alongside the 'main line' for about ½ mile, before rejoining it at the north junction. Both junctions were controlled by ground frames, but these were taken out of use on 4th September 1967, the connections thereafter being worked by hand levers.

About midway between the two junctions, on the eastern side of the line, was Windsor Colliery Platform (11m 74ch). Although constructed in 1943, it was not until 29th October 1951 that this colliers' halt was inspected and approved by Colonel Langley, on behalf of the Minister of Transport. Colonel Langley's report (completed on 8th November) stated:

'This halt was built in 1943 by the Powell Duffryn Colliery Co. for the use of their workmen, in agreement with the Great Western Railway. It consists of a single platform 61 feet long and an open fronted corrugated iron shelter 25 feet by 9 feet, with access through a style to the adjoining colliery; electric lighting has been provided. The platform wall, which is of brick on concrete foundations, and ash covered platform have settled about 6 inches due to mining subsidence, but arrangements are in hand with the National Coal Board to raise the level to the standard 3 feet above the rail.'

Just eight chains beyond the north junction to the Windsor Colliery sidings were the lower points of the loop at Senghenydd station. Although a terminus, Senghenydd (12m 43ch) had the appearance of a passing station, with platforms on each side of the loop. The line itself continued beyond the loop, through a gate, into the Universal Colliery sidings. A tall, brick-built signal box towards the lower end of the loop gave an excellent view of the entire station layout. A trailing crossover between the Up and Down running lines, midway between the signal box and the south end of the station platforms, was added by 1915.

Plate 61 - Windsor Colliery viewed from the 'Rambling 56' excursion of 31st July 1965.

The Aber Branch

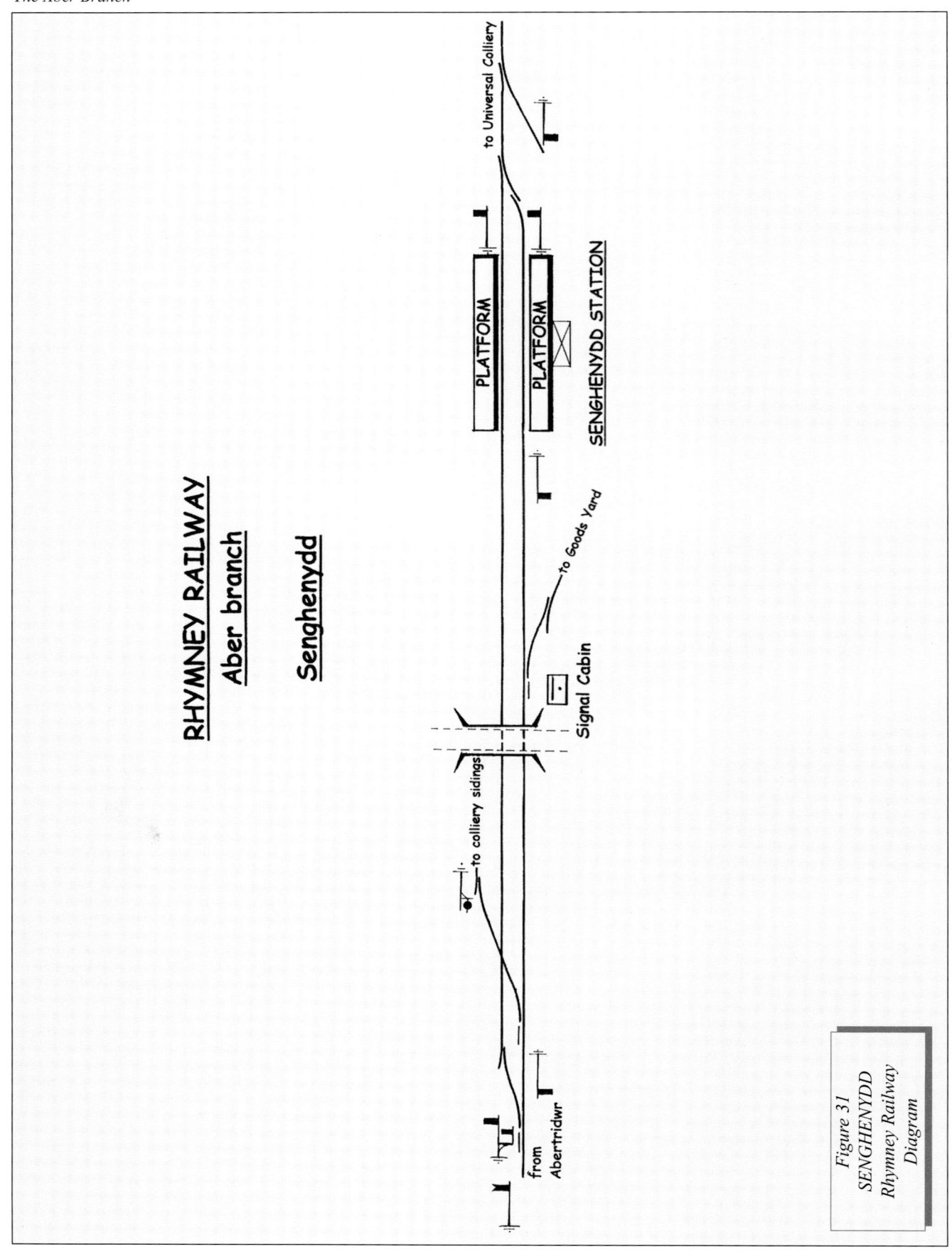

*Figure 31
SENGHENYDD
Rhymney Railway
Diagram*

Figure 32
SENGHENYDD 1928
Signal Box Diagram

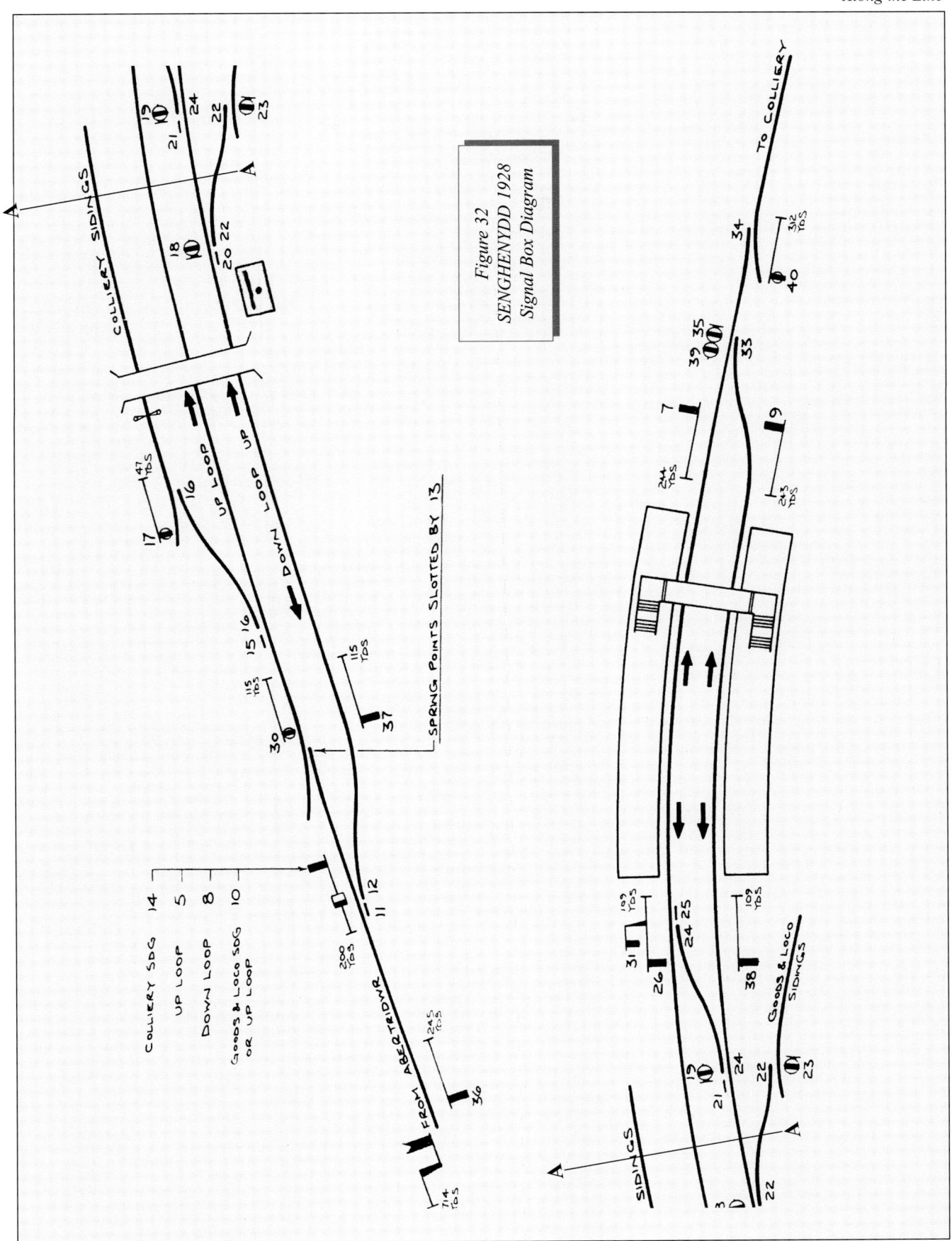

The Aber Branch

Plate 62 - Peckett 0-4-0ST 'Alison' at Windsor Colliery, Abertridwr, on 31st July 1965.

The single-storey stone-built station buildings were situated at about the mid point on the Down platform. No shelter was provided on the Up platform, which was connected to the Down by means of a lattice ironwork footbridge. Following the alteration of the signalling at Senghenydd in 1901 (*see Chapter Three*) most passenger trains arrived and departed from the Down platform, although the former remained fully signalled. There were starting signals at the upper ends of both platforms. In later years the only use for these signals was to permit the engine to run to the dead-end beyond the loop, before running round its train.

The gradient approaching Senghenydd was 1 in 49. In recognition of the inclination through the station itself the Appendix to the Working Timetable (November 1926) contained the following special instructions for working passenger trains at the station:

'Vehicles Standing on Down Platform Loop at Senghenydd Station

When an Up Passenger Train arrives at the Down Platform at Senghenydd Station, the Engine must not be detached from the Train until the hand brakes in the Guards' Vans have been applied and the signal has been lowered for the Engine to go over the points to run round the Train. In windy weather hand scotches must be used in addition to the hand brakes to secure the Train. The Guard will be responsible for observing these instructions.

No vehicles must be left unattached to an Engine on the Down Platform Loop excepting for an Engine to run round a Train, and the Engine must be attached to the vehicles immediately it has run round.

When a vehicle has to be detached from the rear of the Train the Engine must be run round the Train before the vehicle is detached.'

On 12th October 1953 authority was given to abandon the Up platform and to remove the footbridge at Senghenydd. West of this platform was the site of the former loaded wagon sidings for the Universal Colliery.

The connection to the goods yard and locomotive depot trailed away from the Down line near the signal box. This line then curved away to the east before passing over the footpath approach to the passenger station by means of a stone and brick arched bridge. Just beyond this bridge a siding went off to serve the goods shed, a substantial stone-built structure. A loop siding enabled shunting operations to proceed without interfering with the shed road, whilst

Along the Line

Plate 63 - Senghenydd station and disused signal box on 28th September 1963. By this date all lines except the running line had been taken out of use.
Plate 64 - The single running line and disused signal box at Senghenydd after the loop and sidings had been lifted.

77

The Aber Branch

(Above) Plate 65 - The tranquil rural scene above Penyrheol, taken from the overbridge to the west of the halt, as a Senghenydd train departs on 12th May 1952.
(Below) Plate 66 - The end of the line in late 1964 after withdrawal of the passenger service.

another siding alongside the latter was used for stabling carriages in Rhymney Railway days. Goods facilities also included a long siding at the rear of the yard, usually used for general merchandise traffic.

The locomotive depot was situated to the east of the goods yard. It was much more substantial than one would expect for a branch terminus, and at its peak is said to have had an allocation of thirty six engines. The shed itself was a two-road affair, built of stone with a gabled slated roof, measuring about 120ft by 30ft. A large water tank was provided at its rear. The engine shed was demolished in late 1933, leaving only the water tower standing. A siding to the east of the locomotive shed roads had served a large coal stage. All of the sidings that had served the depot had been lifted by 1949.

In June 1955 a further bout of track recovery took place, leaving only the goods shed road and long siding in place in the goods yard. This, coupled with the earlier demolitions and reductions left the whole area looking very derelict, an impression which was not helped by the continuing presence nearby of the rusting pit head gear at the former Universal Colliery. The remaining sidings, together with the run round loop, were taken out of use on 17th February 1963, the day the signal box was closed, and were removed in March of the following year. This left only the single line past the Down platform - the archetypal 'basic railway' - in place for the last few months of the passenger train service.

Plate 67 - The branch dmu at Caerphilly ......

The last day of the passenger train service, 13th June 1964

Plate 68 - ...... and at Senghenydd, awaiting departure.

The Aber Branch

Private and Not for Publication. Notice No. W.4112.

GREAT WESTERN RAILWAY.

SIGNAL ALTERATIONS—SENGHENYDD.

On **WEDNESDAY, AUGUST 30th, 1944**, between the hours of **8.0 a.m** and **4.0 p.m.**, or until the work is completed, the Signal Engineer will be engaged **bringing into use** the undermentioned Independent discs :—

At points leading from Goods Shed to Down Line.

At Catchpoints in Up Loop.

The existing elevated discs at these points will be **taken out of use**.

District-Inspector ROSSER to make all arrangements for safe working, including the appointment of Hand Signalman, and the disconnection of Distant Signals, in accordance with Rule 77.

PLEASE NOTE, ADVISE ALL CONCERNED, AND ACKNOWLEDGE RECEIPT ON FORM BELOW.

H. H. PHILLIPS,
Divisional Superintendent.

CARDIFF.
August 24th, 1944.

Figure 33 - Great Western Railway Circular W4112 for work at Senghenydd in 1944. This involved the bringing into use of two Independent discs.

Notice No. W.1507.

SIGNAL ALTERATIONS
SENGHENYDD.

On **WEDNESDAY, May 28th, 1947**, between the hours of **9.0 a.m.** and **4.0 p.m.**, or until the work is completed, the Signal Department will be engaged **bringing into use** the undermentioned Independent Disc :—

Form.	Description.	Position.	Distance from Box.
1	1. Up to Down Loop	Up Side of Up Loop	84 Yards.
2	2. Backing Down Up Loop.	Up Side of Up Loop.	

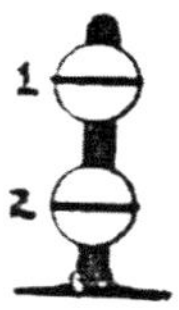

The following Signals will be **taken out of use**:—
Up to Down Loop Starting.
Elevated Disc Backing Down Up Loop.

District Inspector ROSSER to make all arrangements for safe working, including the appointment of the necessary handsignalmen, and disconnection of Distant Signals in accordance with Rule 77.

H. H. SWIFT,
Divisional Superintendent.

CARDIFF,
May 21st, 1947.

Figure 34 - An extract from Great Western Railway Circular W1507 for the bringing into use of two Independent discs and removal of two other signals at Senghenydd in May 1947.

This particular circular also carried details of work at Ystrad Mynach.

7
Postscript

South Wales has witnessed a remarkable revival in the fortunes of a number of local passenger services withdrawn during and after the Beeching years. Passenger trains once again run to Aberdare and Maesteg and call at local stations between Cardiff and Swansea, while a completely new service operates between Radyr and Cardiff Central, via Ninian Park (the 'City Line').

If the Caerphilly to Senghenydd passenger train service had survived the closures of 1964 then it, like the Coryton branch, could now be fulfilling a worthwhile role as part of an expanded Valley Lines network. On the basis of the current timetable it could have formed an extension of the Cardiff to Caerphilly workings, providing what the branch never achieved in its lifetime - a regular interval through service between the Aber Valley and Cardiff. Unfortunately, the closure of the Windsor Colliery and the subsequent abandonment of the branch came too early for the line to benefit from the expansionist period which blossomed from the mid 1980s.

Today significant parts of the Aber branch have been taken for redevelopment, including Senghenydd and Abertridwr station sites and land formerly occupied by sidings at Aber junction. Intervening sections of the former line still survive but the overall continuity of the route has now been lost. This, perhaps, is the greatest tragedy. As events elsewhere have shown, closure and even track removal are not necessarily irreversible. Failure, to safeguard the continuity of the route, on the other hand, means that the opportunity to reinstate the line has now disappeared, probably for ever. This short-sighted policy has now been reversed, but for the Aber branch this change has clearly come too late.

Plate 69 - A handful of passengers make use of the doomed service from Senghenydd in 1963. The line had been singled by then and any redundant trackwork lifted.

The Aber Branch

APPENDIX 1 - SUMMARY of TRAFFIC at STATIONS on the ABER BRANCH
From: 'Traffic Dealt with at Stations and Goods Depots, 1903-38' (GWR 1938/39)

	STAFF.			PASSENGER TRAIN TRAFFIC					
							Parcels and Miscellaneous		
YEAR	Supervisory and Wages (all grades)	Paybill Expenses	TOTAL RECEIPTS	Tickets Issued	Season Tickets	Passenger Receipts (including S.T. etc.)	Number	Receipts	Total
	No.	£	£	No.	No.	£	No.	£	£

Senghenydd — Taken over from the Rhymney Railway, January, 1922.

1923	36	5,251	11,312	189,041	256	5,297	14,433	268	5,565
1929	29	3,343	4,678	24,074	533	2,605	8,354	233	2,838
1930	27	3,196	3,920	20,902	487	1,951	7,084	206	2,157
1931	11	2,227	2,654	19,562	402	1,779	6,499	184	1,963
1932	+17	2,545	2,115	19,455	484	1,962	6,212	153	2,115
1933	+16	2,385	2,055	21,363	372	1,899	7,636	156	2,055
1934	8	1,291	2,090	17,415	488	1,957	6,751	133	2,090
1935	8	1,178	2,313	19,281	401	2,268	6,814	45	2,313
1936	8	1,193	2,341	18,676	421	2,290	6,338	51	2,341
1937	8	1,210	2,403	18,232	555	2,341	6,686	62	2,403
1938	8	1,235	1,935	16,492	397	1,880	7,253	55	1,935

Abertridwr — Taken over from the Rhymney Railway, January, 1922.

1923	10	1,444	10,202	79,942	229	3,856	16,432	336	4,192
1929	12	1,463	7,682	35,440	908	3,684	10,609	237	3,921
1930	11	1,543	7,067	25,727	832	2,823	10,292	247	3,070
1931	10	1,249	5,681	26,171	944	2,590	9,401	193	2,783
1932	*	*	2,665	23,917	1,019	2,454	8,989	211	2,665
1933	*	*	2,457	24,210	750	2,248	10,769	209	2,457
1934	8	1,031	2,705	22,593	947	2,497	9,962	208	2,705
1935	7	1,019	2,734	27,148	938	2,635	10,069	99	2,734
1936	7	1,032	2,878	28,033	1,006	2,772	10,716	106	2,878
1937	7	1,042	2,677	27,621	984	2,596	10,012	81	2,677
1938	7	1,071	2,545	23,369	1,015	2,477	9,922	68	2,545

Penyrheol — Taken over from the Rhymney Railway, January, 1922.

1923	8	1,033	1,946	67,056	115	1,435	1,777	77	1,512
1929	6	779	482	7,031	175	433	811	49	482
1930	4	440	242	2,990	139	216	400	26	242

Made a 'halt' under Caerphilly, August 1930.

* Included with Senghenydd
\+ Includes Abertridwr in 1932 and 1933

APPENDIX 1 - SUMMARY of TRAFFIC at STATIONS on the ABER BRANCH
From: 'Traffic Dealt with at Stations and Goods Depots, 1903-38' (GWR 1938/39)

GOODS TRAIN TRAFFIC

	Forwarded			Received							
	Coal and Coke "Charged"	Other Minerals	General Merchandise	Coal and Coke "Charged"	Other Minerals	General Merchandise	Coal and Coke "Not Charged" (Forw'd and Rec'd)	Total Goods Tonnage	Total Receipts (Exc."Not Charged" Coal and Coke)	Livestock (Forw'd and Rec'd)	Total Carted Tonnage (included in Total Goods Tonnage)
	Tons	Tons	Tons	Tons	Tons	Tons	Tons	Tons	£	Wagons	Tons
Senghenydd *(cont)*											
(1923)	207	869	210	153	2,936	9,836	#414,175	428,386	5,747	3	1,524
(1929)	-	669	240	395	123	1,228	#6,215	8,870	1,840	3	769
(1930)	-	549	1,310	912	280	1,110	#5,387	9,548	1,763	2	607
(1931)	-	154	283	46	43	522	#3,265	4,313	691	-	257

Included with Caerphilly Goods after 1931.

Abertridwr *(cont)*											
(1923)	22	322	184	312	3,976	12,811	#328,956	346,583	6,010	49	1,384
(1929)	525	339	458	1,898	1,904	14,357	#376,235	395,716	3,761	24	708
(1930)	1,716	309	307	2,784	1,381	14,630	#329,554	350,681	3,997	28	510
(1931)	5,003	90	72	97	572	6,520	#145,841	158,195	2,898	17	277

Included with Caerphilly Goods after 1931.

Penyrheol *(cont)*											
(1923)	-	85	258	-	179	274	#9	805	434	8	145

Included with Caerphilly Goods after 1928.

\# Includes "Permitted" traffic.

Appendix 2
Bridge and Demolition Notes

From 1975 onwards Alastair Warrington was a Senior Technical Officer in the Bridge Section of British Rail's Divisional Civil Engineer's Office at Newport. Soon after the closure of the line, on 26th September 1977, he walked it with John Sharpe, a Senior Technical Officer in the Permanent Way Section.

The purpose of the visit was to categorise the permanent way for the removal contract and to include the metallic superstructures of as many bridges as possible. The walk was from Senghenydd to Aber Junction and the three pages of diagrams show the state of the line at that time.

Bridges included in the demolition contract were Occupation underbridges Nos.3 and 4, at 10m 08¼c and 10m 35c respectively, the three span Aber Viaduct (bridge No.9) at 11m 44c, and Pond underbridge (No.10) at 11m 48½c, as well as the BR portion of the colliery road overbridge (No.11) at 11m 71c. The contract was not let for some while as the tenders had to be invited by British Rail's Supplies & Contracts Manager at Derby.

The National Coal Board demolished the former colliery tramway overbridges at 11m 65¾c, 11m 67¼c and 11m 68½c during 1978, as well as their portion of the overbridge at 11m 71c. Demolition of the track started on 11th September 1978 at the Penyrheol end and a short section of track had been removed at that end of the line on that date. By 8th November 1978 all track had been removed except between the two overbridges south of Abertridwr station.

The superstructures of the three small underbridges and the colliery overbridge at 11m 71c had all been removed by February 1979, and demolition of Aber Viaduct had just commenced. Four days later, on 6th February 1979, demolition was in progress and, by the following day, four of the six girders had been dropped. The two girders over the road were removed on 25th February 1979, the demolition being carried out by Messrs T W Ward.

Plate 70 - Demolition of the Aber Viaduct, Bridge No.9 at 11m 44c, in February 1979.

Plate 71 - The line across the Aber Viaduct, on 26th September 1977.

Appendix 2

To Abertridwr ↑

S P (removed)

Public road

(No.9)   11m 44c Aber Viaduct
3-span underbridge carrying single line over public road and brook. 37ft 9in span over road; 38ft 4in over brook; 37ft 8in over vacant ground. Six plate girders, cross girders and flat plate flooring, railbearers, masonry abutments piers and wing walls. Steel rail parapet. 2ch long. 1891.

Aber Viaduct; Remove steelwork, demolish pilasters & 2 No. piers; fence across abutments.

Gate removed

Pond U B; Remove steelwork, demolish pilasters, fence across abutments.

(No.10)   11m 48½c Pond Bridge
Single 69ft 8in span Occupation underbridge carrying single line over pond. Two steel plate girders, flat plate flooring, one bar parapet rail, Deck type, masonry abutments and wings, large wall built by Colliery Company alongside on left (West) of track.

Siding lifted

N C B Loco gone from here to Mountain Ash

11m 65¾c Footbridge
Single 43ft 11in span colliery overbridge over single line. Steel girders and steel braced columns, two or three spans over colliery sidings. Windsor Colliery Company.

N C B overbridge

N C B overbridge

11m 67¼c Footbridge
Single 44ft span colliery overbridge as above.

11m 68½c Footbridge
Single 44ft 6in span colliery overbridge as above.

N C B overbridge

WINDSOR COLLIERY HALT (11m 73¼c)

Occupation L C

Still in situ

BRIDGE and DEMOLITION DETAILS

The notes on the left of the track diagrams are taken from the Bridge Register; those on the right are the September 1977 notes made by Alastair Warrington in his official capacity when he walked the line shortly after its closure.
Not all entries in the Bridge Register are reproduced.

Remains of N C B diesel loco (cab) here

NCB sidings lifted

Gate removed

(No.12)   12m 21¼c Occupation bridge
Single 7ft 8in span Occupation underbridge under single line. Two shallow plate girders under rails, flat plate flooring. Masonry abutments and wing walls. Note: This bridge was extended on the West side with square trough flooring for Colliery Sidings, but never used.

C P spiked out of use

Rhymney Railway chairs

12/1

Sidings never put in

End of rails

(No.13)   12m 35c Parc-newydd Bridge
Single 47ft span public overbridge over four lines. Two plate girders, cross girders with buckled floor plates, plate parapets 20ft 1in apart. Masonry abutments and wings (box on West side). Notice Plate: District Traffic notice. Road surface maintained by Caerphilly UDC.

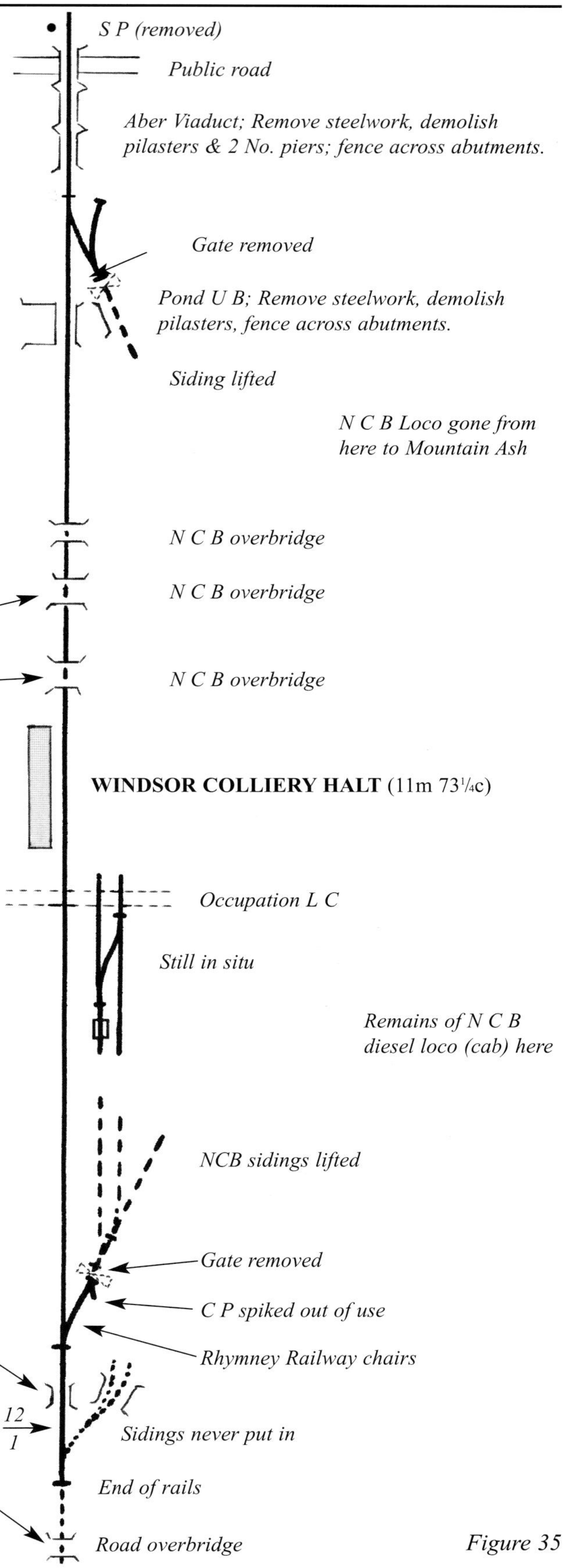

Road overbridge

Figure 35

The Aber Branch

To Penyrheol

(No.2) 9m 71¼c Furness Road Bridge
Single 23ft 8in span (27ft 11in on skew) public bridge over single line. Segmental masonry arch, masonry abutments, wings and parapets 25ft apart. Road surface maintained by Caerphilly UDC.

O B

(No.3) 10m 08¾c Occupation Bridge
Single 11ft 10in span occupation underbridge under single line. Two shallow steel girders under rails, flat plate flooring, one bar parapet rail, masonry abutments and wings.

U B 10m 08¼c
To be removed and abutments fenced

10m 12¼c 'Old Mill Race'
Single 4ft span (disused) tramway underbridge under single line. Two ring brick arch, masonry walls.

U B 10m 12¼cc
Disused tramway formation

(No.4) 10m 35¾c Occupation Bridge
Single 14ft 11in span occupation underbridge under single line. Two shallow plate girders, square trough flooring, masonry abutments and wings, one bar parapet rail.

U B 10m 35c
To be removed and abutments fenced

> ** Bridge No.7: The stonework and brickwork of Bridge No.7 which, in 2001, was owned and maintained by the Strategic Rail Authority, was repointed as recently as May 2001. However, repainting of the rusty steel parapets is not planned for the foreseeable future, much to the chagrin of the local residents!*

(No.6) 11m 02¼c Abertridwr Mill
Single 29ft 9½in span public path over single line. Four shallow plate girders, three brick jack arches (6in water pipe under one), masonry abutments, wings and parapets 12ft apart. Notice Plates: 3 Ton axle load sign and 'Ordinary' Traffic sign.

O B 11m 02¼c (Occupation)

* (No.7) 11m 20¼c Groeswen Road
Single 24ft 11in span (37ft 10in on skew) public bridge over single line. Two plate girders, plate parapets 20ft 5in apart. Cross girders and brick jack arches, masonry abutments and wings. Notice Plates: 3 Ton axle load sign and 'Ordinary' Traffic sign.

O B

O B 11m 21½c Aqueduct

11m 21½c Aqueduct
Three-span aqueduct over double line. 1st span 22ft 1in, 2nd span 27ft 4in, 3rd span 19ft 5in. Steel plate trough 1ft 6in wide, 1ft 3in deep (inside), masonry abutments, timber piers (braced).

Site of S B (removed)

ABERTRIDWR (11m 35c)

11m 36¾c Station footbridge
Single 39ft 6in span station footbridge over double line. Light lattice girders on iron columns, timber flooring steps, 4ft 3in wide. Removed 1968.

From Senghenydd

Figure 36

Appendix 2

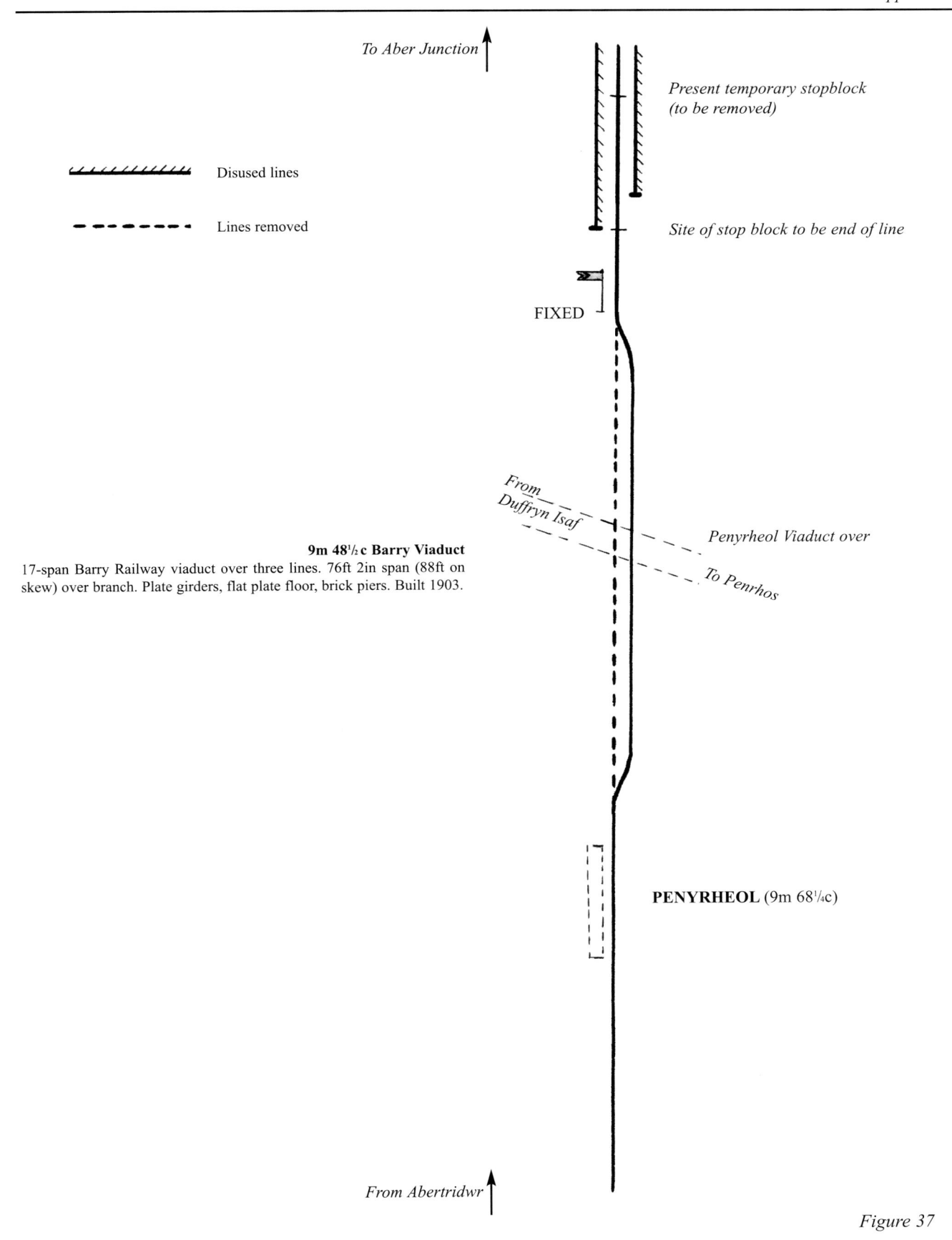

━━━━━━━━━━━ Disused lines

━ ━ ━ ━ ━ Lines removed

To Aber Junction ↑

Present temporary stopblock (to be removed)

Site of stop block to be end of line

FIXED

From Duffryn Isaf

Penyrheol Viaduct over

To Penrhos

9m 48½c Barry Viaduct
17-span Barry Railway viaduct over three lines. 76ft 2in span (88ft on skew) over branch. Plate girders, flat plate floor, brick piers. Built 1903.

PENYRHEOL (9m 68¼c)

From Abertridwr ↑

Figure 37

87

The Aber Branch

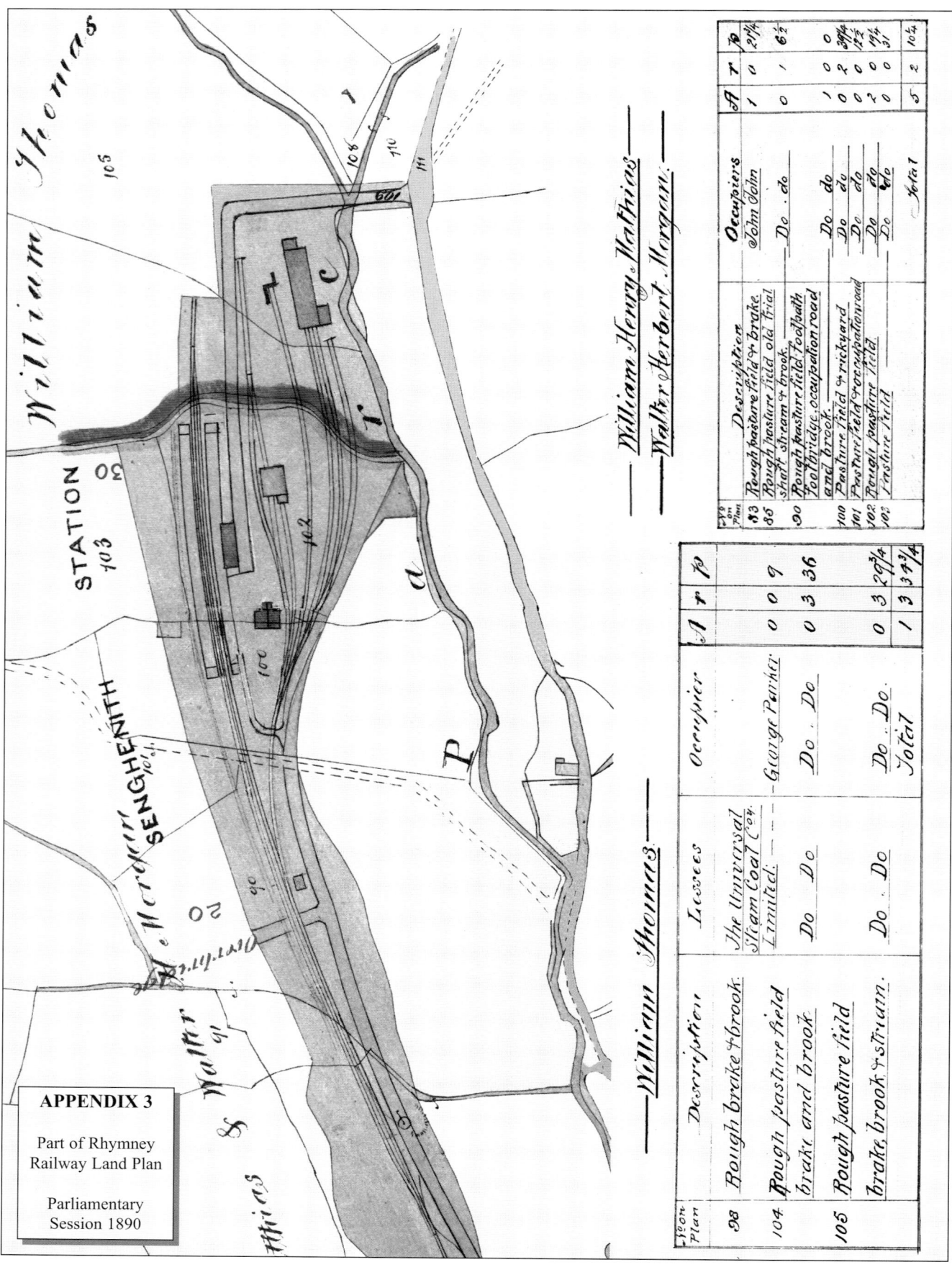

APPENDIX 3

Part of Rhymney Railway Land Plan

Parliamentary Session 1890

— *William Thomas* —

No on Plan	Description	Lessees	Occupier	A	r	p
98	Rough brake & brook	The Universal Steam Coal Cov. Limited	George Parker	0	0	9
104	Rough pasture field brake and brook	Do Do	Do Do	0	3	36
105	Rough pasture field brake, brook & stream	Do Do	Do Do	0	3	29¾
			Total	1	3	34¾

— *William Henry Mathias* —
— *Walker Herbert Morgan* —

No on Plan	Description	Occupiers	A	r	p
83	Rough pasture field & brake	John John	1	0	0
85	Rough pasture field old Trial shaft stream & brook	Do do	0	1	6½
90	Rough pasture field, footbath, footbridge, occupation road and brook	Do do	1	0	30¾
100	Pasture field & brickyard	Do do	0	2	12½
101	Pasture field & occupation road	Do do	0	0	19¼
102	Rough pasture field	Do do	2	0	3¼
103	Pasture field	Do do			
		Total	5	2	10¼

Appendix 4
Colliery Notes

UNIVERSAL COLLIERY (notes from Richard Davies)

Description

Senghenydd, Caerphilly, Glamorgan. OS ref. ST 113 912

A medium size colliery located at the head of Aber Valley, 650ft above Sea Level on the slopes of Mynydd Eglwysilan, ten miles north of Cardiff.

Building started - 1891   Production - 1897

Ownership

Date	Owners
	Universal Steam Coal Company
1905	Lewis Merthyr Consolidated Collieries Ltd.
1931	Powell Duffryn Steam Coal Company Ltd.
April 1935	Powell Duffryn Associated Collieries Ltd.
25th March 1944	
	Powell Duffryn Limited
1st January 1947	
	NCB No.7 (South Western) Division; No.5 (Rhymney) Area, No.4 Group
26th March 1967	NCB East Wales Area
1st July 1972	NCB South Wales Area

Notes

The Colliery suffered its first underground explosion on 24th May 1901 claiming 81 lives; a second explosion on 14th October 1913 claimed 439 miners (together with one surface worker), the worst mining disaster in the British Isles.

The closed Colliery was taken over by Powell Duffryn in 1931 to aid in the ventilation of their adjacent Windsor Colliery, Abertridwr but no coal was raised at Universal.

The British Railways connections were removed by 1951.

The disused buildings and winding gear were cleared, some using explosive charges laid by the Royal Engineers (Monmouthshire Militia), during March 1963.

The shafts were filled (using part of the spoil tip) and capped during summer 1979 as they affected the air flow in the newly merged Windsor/Nantgarw Collieries.

Post Closure

Western Softwood built a Sawmill on the Colliery site in 1965.

Both the lamp room and Colliery offices survived the 1963 clearance; the former succumbed during the 1990s whilst the latter was being rebuilt in 2000.

A Memorial to the Senghenydd Mining disaster was erected in a nearby park during 1981.

Former Colliery Officials' residences (Universal Villas) are now in private ownership.

WINDSOR COLLIERY (notes from Richard Davies)

Description

Abertridwr, CAERPHILLY, Glamorgan OS ref. ST 117 898

A medium size Colliery located on the Western side of Aber Valley, 575ft above Sea Level on the slopes of Cefn Eglwysilan, nine miles north of Cardiff.

Building started - September 1897 Production - 1903

Ownership

Date	Owners
August 1896	Windsor Steam Coal Company Limited (connections with George Insole & Son)
1st July 1901	Windsor Steam Coal Company (1901) Ltd.
June 1925	Powell Duffryn Steam Coal Company Ltd.
April 1935	Powell Duffryn Associated Collieries Ltd.
25th March 1944	
	Powell Duffryn Limited
1st January 1947	
	NCB No.7 (South Western) Division; No.5 (Rhymney) Area, No.4 Group
26th March 1967	NCB East Wales Area
1st July 1972	NCB South Wales Area

Notes

Unadvertised GWR-built Workmen's platform, Windsor Colliery Halt, was adjacent to colliery. When the Washery closed c.1974 coal was taken by rail to Nantgarw Colliery for washing.

The BR line was taken out of use 10th January 1977, closing on 5th September 1977.

The last standard gauge NCB locomotive scrapped May 1977.

In 1947 the colliery employed 863. The workforce peaked in 1954 at 1,073 (299,000 tons output) dropped to 566 in 1974 but rose again to 650 in 1979 after the merger with Nantgarw.

Modernisation

A £1.5 million scheme to link Windsor with Nantgarw (2½ miles to the south-west) to form a single streamlined unit started in 1974. Production stopped at Nantgarw and its work-force was transferred to Windsor.

A ¾ mile underground connection was made with Nantgarw on 5th July 1976.

The collieries were merged from December 1976 when mining was concentrated underground at Windsor; coal, materials and men were wound at Nantgarw with Windsor being retained for pumping and ventilation.

Universal shafts were filled and capped during Summer 1979 as they affected the air flow at the merged collieries.

The Aber Branch

(Above) Plate 72 - A dmu approaches Penyrheol on a glorious last day of May in 1962, some two years prior to the withdrawal of the passenger service.

(Left) Plate 73 - The ultimate passenger train from Senghenydd, now just a single line, on 13th June 1964, the last day of the service.

Index

	Page
Aber (*see also* Abertridwr)	12, 15
Aber branch	
Abandonment (1870)	5
Act of Parliament (1864)	4
Act of Parliament (1890)	8
Demolition	84 - 87
Dieselisation	42, 57
Final Closure	44, 84
Inspection	10
Opening	11, 48
Withdrawal of passenger service	43
Aber Junction	5, 15, 20, 33, 40, 44, 59, 64
Aber Junction Halt (*see also* Beddau Halt)	34, 42, 44, 59
Aber Valley Anti Railway Closure Committee	42
Abertridwr (*see also* Aber)	15, 26, 38, 70, 71
Accident	59
Albion Steam Coal Co.	8
Alexandra (Newport & South Wales) Docks & Ry.	24
Auto-trains	50, 54, 55, 57
Barry Railway	8, 15, 24, 26
Beddau Halt (*see also* Aber Junction Halt)	22, 34, 50
Beddau Loop	20, 22, 36, 44
Beeching Report	42, 71
Bell, J	15
Board of Trade	5, 10, 12, 14, 15, 19, 20, 22, 24, 25, 26
Brecon & Merthyr Railway	3, 15, 24, 36, 50
Caerphilly	2, 15, 22, 25, 50, 62
Caerphilly branch	2, 5, 25
Caerphilly tunnel	5, 8
Caerphilly Urban District Council	34
Cardiff & Caerphilly Railway (1860)	3
Cardiff & Caerphilly Railway (1862)	3
Cardiff Caerphilly & Aber Railway	3, 4
Cardiff Division	34
Cardiff Valleys Division	34
Cilfynydd	8
Coalfield	1

	Page
Collieries	
Albion	8
Gwaun Gledyr	5
Llanbradach	8, 14, 55
Nantgarw	44, 89
Penyrheol	4, 64
Tir Gibbon	64
Universal	8, 10, 12, 13, 14, 19, 20, 26, 38, 44, 51, 78, 89
Windsor	13, 14, 15, 19, 26, 35, 40, 43, 44, 51, 58, 59, 73, 89
Contractors	
Allen, J	15
Davies, T W	9, 20
Marnes Chaplin & Co.	25
Symes, W A	20
Ward, T W	84
Cubitt, J	2, 4
Dannett, E H	34
Development (Loan Guarantees and Grants) Act 1929	38
East Glamorgan Railway	14
Energlyn	26, 34, 36
Enthusiasts' excursions	58
Geology	1
Glamorgan County Council	24
Gledyr branch	4, 5, 8, 9
Grouping	33, 54
Insole, J & F	14
Jellicoe Specials	33
Lewis Merthyr Consolidated Collieries Ltd.	8, 89
Lewis, W T (Lord Merthyr of Senghenydd)	8, 32
Locomotive, carriage and wagon manufacturers	
Beyer, Peacock & Co.	54
Cravens Ltd.	49

Hudswell, Clarke & Co.	49	Railway Executive Committee	32, 38
Metropolitan Carriage & Wagon Co.	48	Rhymney Valley & Cardiff Railway	
Neilson, Reid	54	Rhymney Railway	2, 8, 9, 10, 14, 22, 26, 33, 34
R Stephenson & Co.	49, 54		36, 48, 49
Sharp, Stewart & Co.	48, 54	Rhymney Valley & Cardiff Railway	2
Vulcan Foundry	48, 51, 54	Riches, C H	49
Lord Windsor	3	Rumney Railway	2
Lundie, C	14, 22, 49		
		Senghenydd (Senghenith)	10, 14, 15, 19, 26, 36, 42
McKenzie & Holland	12, 20		43, 73, 76
Minister of Transport	36, 38, 42, 43, 73	Senghenydd engine shed	14, 38, 54, 78
		Steam railcars	22, 24, 49, 50, 51
Nationalisation	42		
		Taff Vale Railway	2, 3, 8
Parade (Cardiff)	37	Traffic statistics	82
Penarth Harbour Dock & Railway	8	Transport Users Consultative Committee	43
Penyrheol	15, 35, 42, 70		
Penyrheol Viaduct	15, 36, 70	Universal Steam Coal Co.	8, 9, 89
Powell Duffryn Steam Coal Co.	35, 89		
Prosser, E	22, 32, 33, 49	Wainwright, F G	34
		Western Welsh Omnibus Co.	34
Radyr engine shed	38, 57	Windsor Colliery Platform	40, 73
Railhead Distribution	36	Windsor Steam Coal Co.	14, 19, 51, 89

Sources and Bibliography

Research for this book has largely been based on primary source material and contemporary journals. Information from company minute books and reports and from Board of Trade inspections and other documents has come from the Public Record Office at Kew. Private and Local Acts, Parliamentary Notices in *The London Gazette*, British Railways, GWR and Bradshaws timetables, and journals such as the *Railway Times*, *Railway News*, and the *Great Western Railway Magazine* have been consulted at Leicester University Library. Contemporary newspapers, including the *Cardiff & Merthyr Guardian*, the *Cardiff Times* and the *Western Mail*, were inspected at Cardiff Central Library. The *Railway Observer* provided very useful details of more recent events.

Books consulted include:

Caerphilly Works 1901-1964,	E R Mountford; Roundhouse Books, 1965
Cardiff and the Marquesses of Bute,	J Davies; University of Wales Press, 1981
The Great Western at War 1939-1945,	T Bryan; Patrick Stephens, 1995
Great Western Auto Trailers, Vols. 1 and 2,	J Lewis; Wild Swan, 1991and 1995
History of the Great Western Railway,	E T MacDermot; GWR, 1927
Locomotive and Train Working in the Latter Part of the 19th Century, E L Ahrons; Heffer, 1923	
The Locomotives of the GWR, Part 10,	The Railway Correspondence and Travel Society
A Register of GWR Absorbed Coaching Stock 1922/23, E R Mountford; The Oakwood Press, 1978	
Rhondda Coal, Cardiff Gold,	R Watson; Merton Priory Press, 1997
The Rhymney Railway,	D S Barrie; The Oakwood Press, 1963
The Valley in the Shadow,	J H Brown; 1981